STITCHERS

by Esther Freud

Premiered at Jermyn Street Theatre

30 May – 23 June 2018

Press performance Friday 1 June

SAMUEL FRENCH

samuelfrench.co.uk

STITCHERS

Premiered at the Jermyn Street Theatre, London on 30 May 2018 with the following cast:

CAST

LADY ANNE TREE	Sinéad Cusack
BUSBY	Martin Docherty
DENISE	Victoria Elizabeth
LEN	Trevor Laird
ŁUKASZ	Michael Nardone
KEITH	Ewan Stewart
TOMMY	Frankie Wilson

CREATIVES

Writer	Esther Freud
Director	Gaby Dellal
Designer	Liz Cooke
Lighting Designer	Will Reynolds
Sound Designer	Max Pappenheim
Co-producer	Molly Eagles
Movement Director	Cydney Uffindell-Phillips
Assistant Director	Molly Eagles
Musical Supervisor	Stephen Hiscock
Fight Director	Philip d'Orléans
Stage Manager	Amy Spall
Production Manager	Matt Tarbuck
Assistant Stage Manager	Molly Jackson-French
Production Intern	Holly Tilt
Production Photographer	Robert Workman

Produced and general managed by Jermyn Street Theatre

With thanks to Stag & Bow, LoveCrafts, MacCulloch & Wallis
Set constructed by Rupert Blakeley at Oxford Theatre Workshops

AUTHOR'S NOTE

I've been a supporter of Fine Cell Work since its inception, but it was only once I had the idea of writing a play about prisoners stitching that I became actively involved.

My first prison visit was to the Isle of Wight. The volunteer I accompanied went every fortnight. There was no sewing room, so she walked from wing to wing, handing out wool and kits, offering advice, while I trailed nervously behind. On the second wing a man was waiting for us. "This cream wool," his fury was palpable, "is not the same shade as the cream wool that I've been using." And it was true. He'd been working on a cushion with two artichokes in its centre and now the background was uneven. The volunteer commiserated and promised to reorder, but a look of panic came into his eyes. "What will I do till it arrives?"

"I have five more wings to visit," she stayed calm, "but if there's anything left over at the end of the day..."

"I'll be waiting," he assured her.

As we moved on she whispered that he used to be a self-harmer, but since he had his sewing...

On every wing there were men, thread and kits in hand. Each item they completed fetched them a fee, but it was clear they weren't just there for the money. "It's the only place anyone calls me by my name," one man told me when I asked. Another: "It's the colours, everything else in here is grey." One inmate was stitching for up to forty hours a week. The Christmas before he'd sent his daughters a present. First time in ten years.

At the end of the day there was one kit left, and as we walked out through the prison we saw our man, waiting, his hands stuck through the bars.

"I do have something for you," and then she paused apologetic "although I'm afraid it's a design for *three* artichokes," and he was about to swear when he lifted it in, and thanked her.

Since then I have become a regular visitor at the sewing class at one of London's high-security prisons. What I see there is sobering. Loneliness, violence, despair, but in one small room, on Tuesday afternoons, there is the hum of quiet industry – laughter, chat and the production of astonishingly beautiful work. "I don't know how I'd have got through the sentence without my embroidery," one man told me, and on a recent visit another looked up from a butterfly he was making. "The time flew by!" And a look of amazement crossed his face.

CAST

SINÉAD CUSACK
Lady Anne Tree

Theatre includes: *King Lear* (Chichester Festival Theatre, West End); *Splendour* (Donmar Warehouse) and *Other Desert Cities, The Cherry Orchard, A Winter's Tale* (The Old Vic).

Television includes: *North and South, Moving On* and *Call The Midwife.*

Film includes: *Hoffman, Waterland, Tales from Hollywood, Stealing Beauty, The Tiger's Tail, The Sea* and *Queen and Country.*

MARTIN DOCHERTY
Busby

Theatre includes: *Venice Preserved, Annville, Mcluckies Line, A Family Sentence* (Citizens Theatre); *Risk, Club Asylum, Antigone, Cooking With Elvis* (Tron Theatre); *Decky Does A Bronco-Gridiron, Thieves And Boy-Oran Mor, Continuous Growth, Preen Back Yer Lugs, The Year Of the Hare* (Peoples Theatre Of Finland); *Nasty Brutish and Short* (Traverse Theatre) and *The Hard Man* (Finborough Theatre).

Television includes: *Still Game, Rab C Nesbit, River City, Case Histories, One Night In Emergency, Dear Green Place, Gary Tank Commander* and *Father Brown.*

Film includes: *Tam, I Love Luci, Filth, Cloud Atlas; Marty Goes To Hollywood* – a documentary featuring Martin as himself won a New Talent Bafta in 2015 .

VICTORIA ELIZABETH
Denise

For Jermyn Street Theatre: Richard Leigh's *Late Night Magic.*

Theatre includes: *GRC* (Pleasance Theatre).

Film and television includes: *Not The Devil* that screened at BFI Flare; Dom Joly's *The Complainers*, *Supersize Kids* (ITV).

Victoria is also a professional magician with her own magic and comedy-cabaret act. As an actress she has played all sorts of roles in theatre, boys and girls.

She has also entertained and performed magic at Madame Jojo's and more recently on stage at the Royal Vauxhall Tavern.

TREVOR LAIRD
Len

Theatre includes: *Black Men Walking* (Royal Exchange and National Tour); *One Man Two Guvnors* (National Theatre, West End and Broadway); *Hamlet* (Black Theatre Live); *England People Very Nice*, *Statement of Regret*, *The Mysteries* (National Theatre); *Colors*, *Can't Take It With You* (Abbey Theatre); *Othello* (Tivoli Theatre, Dublin and International Tour); *A Midsummer Night's Dream*, *Twelfth Night* (Regent's Park Open Air Theatre); *Safe in Our Hands*, *Sunsets and Glories*, *Foxes*, *The Revenges Tragedy* (West Yorkshire Playhouse); *Much Ado About Nothing* (Old Vic Theatre) and *Master Harold and the Boys* (Liverpool Everyman Theatre).

Television includes: *No Offence*, *Toast of London* (Channel 4) and *Death in Paradise*, *Doctor Who*, *Holby City*, *Casualty*, *Waking the Dead*, *Undercover Heart*, *Murder Room* and *Victims of Apartheid* (BBC).

Film includes: *Quadrophenia*, *Babylon*, *The Long Good Friday*, *Smack and Thistle*, *Walter*, *Secrets and Lies* and *Love, Honour and Obey.*

He is also a founder member of Black Theatre Cooperative with whom he has acted and directed.

MICHAEL NARDONE
Łukasz

Theatre include: *King Lear*, *Gagarin Way* (National Theatre); *Remembrance Day* (Royal Court); *Victoria* (RSC); *Black Watch* (National Theatre of Scotland); *Knives in Hens*, *The Speculator*, *Europe* (Traverse); *Marriage of Figaro*, *Mirandolina*, *Merlin* (Royal Lyceum) and *Cyrano De Bergerac*, *The Legend of St Julian* (Communicado).
Recent television and film includes: *The Night Manager*, *In Plain Sight*, *Rellik*, *Will*, *Rogue One*, *Whiskey Galore* and *Child 44*.
Radio includes: *Kidnapped*, *King Lear*, *Measure for Measure*.
He has also performed in a number of motion capture video games, most recently portraying Julius Caesar in Assassins Creed Origins.

EWAN STEWART
Keith

Theatre includes: *The Royale* (Bush Theatre); *Let The Right One In*, *In Time O'Strife* (National Theatre of Scotland); *Dunsinane* (RSC); *Jumpy* (Royal Court); *Much Ado About Nothing* (The Globe); *Beautiful Burnout* and *Things I Know To Be True* (Frantic Assembly).

Television includes: *Walter's War*, *River City*, *The Somme*, *The Interceptor* and *Vera*.

Film includes: *Rob Roy*, *Titanic*, *Valhalla Rising*, *Florence Foster Jenkins* and *Hector*.

FRANKIE WILSON
Tommy

Theatre includes: *Hidden* (33% London).
Television includes: *Reg*; *Detectorists*; *Our World War* (BBC); *Black Mirror* (Netflix) and *From Cradle to Grave* Granchester (ITV).
Radio includes: *What Does the K Stand For* (BBC Radio 4)

CREATIVES

ESTHER FREUD

Writer

Esther Freud trained as an actress before writing her first novel, *Hideous Kinky*, which was shortlisted for the John Llewellyn Rhys Prize and made into a film starring Kate Winslet. After publishing her second novel, *Peerless Flats*, she was chosen as one of Granta's Best Young British Novelists. Her other books include *The Sea House* and *Lucky Break*, and her most recent, *Mr Mac and Me*, won Best Novel in the East Anglian Book Awards. She contributes regularly to newspapers and magazines, and teaches creative writing for the Faber Academy.

Stitchers is her first full-length play.

GABY DELLAL

Director

Gaby Dellal's feature film *On a Clear Day* opened The Sundance Film Festival in 2005. Starring Peter Mullan and Brenda Blethyn, Gaby received a Scottish BAFTA for best film/director and Locarno Film Festival's Piazza Grande. Gaby's short *Football* starring Helena Bonham Carter also featured at Sundance. Gaby gave and directed Sienna Miller her first lead in the feature film *Two Wheels Only* and Max Minghella his debut (aged thirteen) in her short film *Toyboys*. Gaby then went on to direct *Tube Tales* starring Rachel Weisz. *Angels Crest* with Elizabeth McGovern, Kate Walsh and Jeremy Piven was in competition at the Tribeca Film Festival 2011. Gaby wrote and directed her most recent feature film *Three Generations* starring Naomi Watts, Elle Fanning and Susan Sarandon, released in 2017, currently available on Netflix.

TV includes the much-acclaimed 3-part TV drama for ITV, *Leaving*, starred Helen McCrory.

Theatre includes: *Ghosts* at the Almeida Theatre, London (associate director). This transferred to the West End, with Lesley Manville, and had a run at BAM (Brooklyn Academy of Music, New York) in 2015.

LIZ COOKE

Designer

Liz has designed extensively for theatre in the UK and abroad. Her credits include: *Talking Heads, A Christmas Carol* (Octagon Bolton); *Peter Pan, Cinderella, Aladdin* (Oxford Playhouse); *The Snow Queen* (Pegasus Theatre); *The Trial of Dennis the Menace* (Southbank Centre); *Othello, The Indian Boy* (RSC); *Bleak House, Humble Boy, The Wicked Lady* (New Vic Theatre); *The Comedy of Errors, Pericles, The Merchant of Venice* (Globe); *Monkey!, The Accrington Pals* (West Yorkshire Playhouse); *Round the Horne – Revisited* (West End and tour); *Shadowmouth* (Sheffield Theatres); *The Birds* (National Theatre); *Ma Vie en Rose* (Young Vic); *Stop Messing About* (Rose Theatre/Leicester Square Theatre/UK tour); *Little Wolf's Book of Badness, The Schuman Plan* (Hampstead Theatre); *The Invention of Love, Touched* (Salisbury Playhouse); *The Glory of Living* (Royal Court); *The Wind and the Willows, Peter Pan, Pirates!* (Polka Theatre); *Les Blancs* (Royal Exchange Theatre); *The Magic Toyshop* (Shared Experience) and *Eldorado* (National Theatre of Prague).

WILLIAM REYNOLDS

Lighting Designer

For Jermyn Street Theatre: *Blinding Light* (lighting), *Bloody Poetry* (set/video) and *Saturday Night* (set/lighting; also Theatre Royal Windsor & Arts Theatre, London)

Upcoming designs include: *Trying It On* (lighting/video – RSC, Royal Court & UK Tour), *Weimar Cabaret* (set/lighting – Barbican Theatre) and *In the Willows* (set/lighting – Exeter Northcott & UK Tour).

Recent designs include: *Sonnet Walks* (Globe Theatre); *Little Mermaid* (set/lighting – Theatre by the Lake & UK Tour); *Jungle Book* (set/lighting – London Wonderground & International Tour); *Blown Away* (set/lighting – Lyric Hammersmith & International Tour); *Radiant Vermin* (set, lighting – Soho Theatre & Brits Off Broadway); *Prima Donna* (video – Sadlers Wells) and *The Gambler* (video – Royal Opera House). William is Artistic Director of Metta Theatre and an Artist in Residence at the V&A Museum.

MAX PAPPENHEIM
Sound Designer

Theatre includes: *The Way of the World* (Donmar Warehouse); *The Children* (Royal Court/Manhattan Theatre Club); *Humble Boy*, The *Lottery of Love, Sheppey, Blue/Heart, Little Light, The Distance* (Orange Tree); *Dry Powder, Sex with Strangers, Labyrinth* (Hampstead); *Ophelias Zimmer* (Schaubühne, Berlin/Royal Court); *Miss Julie* (Theatre by the Lake/Jermyn Street); *The Gaul* (Hull Truck); *Cookies* (Theatre Royal Haymarket); *Teddy, Fabric, Invincible* (National Tours); *Toast* (Park Theatre/59E59 Theaters, New York); *Jane Wenham* (Out of Joint); *Waiting for Godot* (Sheffield Crucible); *My Eyes Went Dark* (Traverse, Edinburgh); *Cargo* (Arcola); *CommonWealth* (Almeida); *Creve Coeur* (Print Room); *Wink* (Theatre503); *Spamalot, The Glass Menagerie* (English Theatre, Frankfurt); *The Cardinal, Kiki's Delivery Service, Fiji Land* (Southwark Playhouse); *Mrs Lowry and Son* (Trafalgar Studios); *Martine, Black Jesus, Somersaults* (Finborough); *The Hotel Plays* (Langham Hotel).

Opera includes: *Miranda* (Opéra Comique, Paris); *Vixen* (Vaults/International Tour); *Carmen:Remastered* (ROH/Barbican).

Radio includes: *Home Front* (BBC Radio 4).
Associate Artist of The Faction and Silent Opera.

CYDNEY UFFINDELL-PHILLIPS
Movement Director

Theatre includes: (as Choreographer/Movement Director): *The Be All and End All* (York Theatre Royal); *Our Country's Good* (Ramps on the Moon); *L'Enfant et les Sortilèges* (Teatro Bacional de São Carlos); *A Christmas Carol* (Creation Theatre, Oxford); *Jekyll and Hyde* (The English Theatre Frankfurt); *The Revengers Tragedy* (Nottingham Playhouse) and *Beauty & the Beast* (Mercury Theatre, Colchester).
(as Associate Choreographer): *Wonder.land* (National Theatre & Théâtre du Châtelet) and *Cabaret* (UK tour).
(as Associate Director): *The Wedding Singer* (UK Tour). Resident Director: *Wind in the Willows* (Vaudeville Theatre).

Television includes: (as Choreographer): *Me & Mrs Jones* (BBC – Hartswood films), *Campus* (Channel 4 – Moniker Pictures) and *Green Wing* (Channel 4 – Talkback Productions).

(as Assistant Choreographer): *Smack the Pony* - Series 2, 3 & Christmas Special (Channel 4 - Talkback Productions).

Film includes: (as Associate Choreographer): *London Road* (BBC - National Theatre - Cuba Pictures).
(as Director/Choreographer): *Thin Air* VR 360 Short Film (Khaki Films).

MOLLY EAGLES

Assistant Director / Co-producer

Molly Eagles studied Creative Writing at UEA and has recently joined theatre company Damsel Productions.
Producer credits include: *Where Are We Now?* (The Old Red Lion Theatre), and *The Naivety: A Journey* (Tabernacle).
Co-producer credits include: *Once Upon a Times Up* (Angel Studios).
Associate Producer credits include: *The Snow Queen* (Tabernacle).
Assistant Producer credits include: *Damsel Develops* (The Bunker Theatre) and *Grotty* (The Bunker Theatre).

STEPHEN HISCOCK

Musical Supervisor

Stephen studied drama at Manchester University before becoming a musician.

Previous work includes: *A Midsummer Night's Dream* and *The Frontline* (2008); *A New World* (2009); *Macbeth* (2010/11); *Dr Faustus* (2011) and *A Comedy of Errors* (2013) at Shakespeare's Globe. Session work includes Squeeze, Aimee Mann, Nanci Griffith and Alison Moyet and he is currently drummer for Mark Eitzel. He's a founder member of Britain's most innovative chamber group, **ensemblebash**, working with musicians such as Stewart Copeland, Steve Reich, Nitin Sawhney, Joanna MacGregor, Nana Vasconcelos, Evelyn Glennie, Django Bates, Kathryn Tickell, Chick Corea and the Pan African Orchestra. He also plays in the retro-futuristic theremin and robot band Spacedog. Also a composer, he's written the score to the feature documentary *Light in the Himalayas* (released 2018) and was the composer and solo onstage musician in Complicite's show *Lionboy* - which toured to Broadway, Seoul, Cape Town and Hong Kong in 2015.

PHILIP D'ORLÉANS
Fight Director

Theatre includes: *Romeo & Juliette* (Korea National Opera); *Titus Andronicus* (RSC); *The Kite Runner* (Wyndham's Theatre); *King Lear* (The Globe); *Cabaret* (National Tour); *Macbeth 1847* (Buxton Opera Festival); *Our Country's Good, The Cherry Orchard, Noises Off* (Nottingham Playhouse); *Brighton Rock* (Theatre Royal York); *Cyrano de Bergerac, King Lear* (Northern Broadsides); *Treasure Island, Robin Hood* (Duke's Theatre); *Jekyll & Hyde* (Frankfurt English Theatre); *Great Expectations* (National Tour); *The Ladykillers* (Hull Truck Theatre); *Treasure Island, Dial M For Murder* (New Vic Theatre); *The Beggar's Opera, Midsummer Night's Dream, Stig of the Dump* (Storyhouse Chester); *Grapes of Wrath, Dedication* (Nuffield Southampton); *Wait Until Dark* (Vienna English Theatre); *Fox on the Fairway* (Queen's Theatre Hornchurch); *Faustus* (Creation Theatre Oslo); *La Scala Di Seta, Der Rosen Kavalier* (Royal Opera House) and *L'Isola Disabitata* (ROH International Tour).

Film includes: *King Arthur: Legend of The Sword* (Warner Bros); *Pan* (Warner Bros) and *The Knife That Killed Me* (Universal Pictures).

JERMYN STREET THEATRE

During the 1930s, the basement of 16b Jermyn Street – close to Piccadilly in the heart of London's West End – was home to the glamorous Monseigneur Restaurant and Club. The space was converted into a theatre by Howard Jameson and Penny Horner in the early 1990s and Jermyn Street Theatre staged its first production in August 1994. The theatre director Neil Marcus became the first Artistic Director in 1995 and secured Lottery funding for the venue; the producer Chris Grady also made a major contribution to the theatre's development. In the late 1990s, the Artistic Director was David Babani, later the founder and Artistic Director of the Menier Chocolate Factory.

Over the last twenty years the theatre has established itself as one of London's leading Off-West End studio theatres, with hit productions including *Barefoot in the Park* with Alan Cox and Rachel Pickup, directed by Sally Hughes, and *Helping Harry* with Adrian Lukis and Simon Dutton, directed by Nickolas Grace.

Gene David Kirk, accompanied by Associate Director Anthony Biggs, became Artistic Director in the late 2000s and reshaped the theatre's creative output with revivals of rarely performed plays, including Charles Morgan's post-war classic *The River Line*, the UK premiere of Ibsen's first performed play *St John's Night*, and another Ibsen, *Little Eyolf* starring Imogen Stubbs and Doreen Mantle. Tom Littler staged two acclaimed Stephen Sondheim revivals: *Anyone Can Whistle*, starring Issy van Randwyck and Rosalie Craig, and *Saturday Night*, which transferred to the Arts Theatre.

In 2012 Trevor Nunn directed the world premiere of Samuel Beckett's radio play *All That Fall* starring Eileen Atkins and Michael Gambon. The production subsequently transferred to the Arts Theatre and then to New York's 59E59 Theatre. Jermyn Street Theatre was nominated for the Peter Brook Empty Space Award in 2011 and won The Stage 100 Best Fringe Theatre in 2012. Anthony Biggs became Artistic Director in 2013, combining his love of rediscoveries with a new focus on emerging artists and writers from outside the UK. Recent revivals include Eugene O'Neill's early American work *The First Man*, Terence Rattigan's first play *First Episode*, John Van Druten's First World War drama *Flowers of the Forest*, and a repertory season of South African drama. New works include US playwright Ruby Rae Spiegel's *Dry Land*, Jonathan Lewis's *A Level Playing Field*, and Sarah Daniels' *Soldiers' Wives* starring Cath Shipton.

Last summer, Anthony Biggs stepped down and Tom Littler took over as Artistic Director. Littler has previously been Associate Director of the new writing venue Theatre503 and Associate Director of the Peter Hall Company. He founded the theatre company Primavera and ran it for over ten years, winning numerous awards. His opening production, the world premiere of Howard Brenton's *The Blinding Light*, was his sixth at Jermyn Street Theatre.

Most recently Littler oversaw the most ambitious project in the theatre's history – the first complete London revival of Noel Coward's nine play cycle *Tonight at 8.30* since 1936. Jermyn Street Theatre's Deputy Director Stella Powell-Jones brought *Tomorrow at Noon* to the stage – three contemporary responses to Coward's work by female playwrights. The two productions ran side-by-side leading to 36 one-plays performed each week with tremendously popular trilogy days on Saturdays and Sundays. Throughout its history, the theatre's founders, Howard Jameson and Penny Horner, have continued to serve as Chair of the Board and Executive Director respectively, and the generous donors, front of house staff, and tireless volunteers all play their parts in the Jermyn Street Theatre story.

SUPPORT JERMYN STREET THEATRE

Everybody needs their best friends, and every theatre needs them too. At Jermyn Street Theatre we have recently started a Director's Circle. Limited to twenty-five individuals or couples, these are the people we rely on most. They sponsor productions, fund new initiatives, and support our staff. It is a pleasure to get to know them: we invite Director's Circle members to our exclusive press nights and parties, and we often have informal drinks or suppers in small groups. They are also an invaluable sounding board for me. Currently, members of the Director's Circle donate between £2,000 and £55,000 (with a threshold of £2,000 to join). They are our heroes and they make everything possible. We have space at the table for more, and I would love to hear from you.

Tom Littler
Artistic Director

THE DIRECTOR'S CIRCLE

Anonymous
Jocelyn Abbey and Tom Carney
Philip and Christine Carne
Colin Clark
Charles Glanville and James Hogan
Marjorie Simonds-Gooding
Martin Ward and Frances Card
Robert Westlake and Marit Mohn

AT JERMYN STREET THEATRE

Honorary Patron	HRH Princess Michael of Kent
Patron	Sir Michael Gambon, CBE
Chair of the Board	Howard Jameson
Artistic Director	Tom Littler
Executive Director	Penny Horner
Deputy Director	Stella Powell-Jones*
General Manager	Will Herman
Press and Marketing Manager	Michael Eppy
Artistic Associate	Natasha Rickman
Trainee Director (Birkbeck College)	Tom McClane-Williamson
Technical Manager	Will Abell
Building Manager	Jon Wadey
CAPA Study Abroad Interns	

*The Deputy Director position is sponsored by the Carne Trust.

Volunteer Duty Managers	Kennedy Bloomer
	Adam Ishaq
	Laura Jury-Hyde
	Pam Keen
	Adam Lilley
	Grace Wessels
Volunteer Bar Staff	Mandy Berger
	Jerry Cox
	Wendy Ann Jefferies
	Deputy Technicians
Deputy Technicians	David Harvey
	Steve Lowe

Find us at
www.jermynstreettheatre.co.uk
@JSTheatre
Box Office: 020 7287 2875
16b Jermyn Street, London SW1Y 6ST

Jermyn Street Theatre is a charitable trust, Registered Charity No.1019755. It receives no regular statutory or Arts Council funding. Ticket sales account for around two-thirds of the costs of each production, with the remainder met through generous private donations, bequests, trusts and foundations, and corporate sponsorship. Subsidising our overheads and our productions requires around £300,000 each year.

WELCOME TO JERMYN STREET THEATRE

Whether you are a regular supporter or you are discovering us for the first time, I hope you enjoy your visit.

I first read *Stitchers* – as I read many scripts – on the train from my home in Cambridge to London. I was just finishing it when we pulled in to King's Cross, and I was so bowled over by what I'd just read that the train was on the point of leaving and heading back to East Anglia before I remembered to disembark. We were in talks about programming the play a few minutes later.

Like all the best drama, *Stitchers* seemed to open a door to a world I knew nothing about, and brought it into my imagination in a way that seemed both frightening and tender. It blends the personal and the political with assurance and poise. We were delighted when Gaby Dellal came on board to direct it, bringing with her a terrific team of designers and a knockout cast.

Producing *Stitchers* will cost around £70,000. Nobody is well paid, but the cast and crew – like everyone who works at Jermyn Street Theatre – are paid a legal wage. That's unusual in theatres of this size. In our tiny 70-seat auditorium we cannot hope to meet those costs from the box office, even if we sell out. So, in the absence of any public funding, we rely on the generosity of trusts and foundations, and individual donors. We think the work we do here is of real value – nurturing new generations of theatre professionals whilst giving a chance for established artists to take risks. If you think so too, and you think you know a way to help us out, do get in touch.

I hope you enjoy *Stitchers* as much as I do, and that we'll see you again at Jermyn Street Theatre very soon.

Tom Littler
Artistic Director

STITCHERS

by Esther Freud

SAMUEL FRENCH

samuelfrench.co.uk

ISBN 978-0-573-11556-1

www.samuelfrench.co.uk
www.samuelfrench.com

FOR AMATEUR PRODUCTION ENQUIRIES

UNITED KINGDOM AND WORLD
EXCLUDING NORTH AMERICA
plays@samuelfrench.co.uk
020 7255 4302/01

Each title is subject to availability from Samuel French, depending upon country of performance.

MUSIC USE NOTE

Licensees are solely responsible for obtaining formal written permission from copyright owners to use copyrighted music in the performance of this play and are strongly cautioned to do so. If no such permission is obtained by the licensee, then the licensee must use only original music that the licensee owns and controls. Licensees are solely responsible and liable for all music clearances and shall indemnify the copyright owners of the play(s) and their licensing agent, Samuel French, against any costs, expenses, losses and liabilities arising from the use of music by licensees. Please contact the appropriate music licensing authority in your territory for the rights to any incidental music.

USE OF COPYRIGHT MUSIC

A licence issued by Samuel French Ltd to perform this play does not include permission to use the incidental music specified in this copy.

Where the place of performance is already licensed by the PERFORMING RIGHT SOCIETY (PRS) a return of the music used must be made to them. If the place of performance is not so licensed then application should be made to the PRS, 2 Pancras Square, London, N1C 4AG.

A separate and additional licence from PHONOGRAPHIC PERFORMANCE LTD, 1 Upper James Street, London W1F 9DE (www.ppluk.com) is needed whenever commercial recordings are used.

WITH THANKS.

I'd like to thank Katy Emck, Victoria Gillies and Katie Steingold from Fine Cell Work, who did so much to facilitate my research. Isabella Tree, who added to many, many drafts with her precision and humour. Matthew Byam Shaw for early encouragement and support, Jeremy Herrin and Ed Hall who gave up precious time to advise me, Patrick Barlow for his generous enthusiasm, Alex Boyt for inside information, Kitty Aldridge for a particularly brilliant note, Xandra Bingley for being there for me from the start, Edward Henry, so generous with his legal knowledge, Erwin James whose acknowledgement means so much, Margie Markwick whose determination got me inside on many prison visits, Molly Eagles for her ingenuity and dedication, and Gaby Dellal whose insight and passion turned the play around on more than one occasion. Also to Julia Sowerbutts and the Ink festival for giving me the chance to workshop an early version, and Helen Atkinson Wood for showing me how it could be done. Also Taz Fustok for the use of his club, Laylow, Jacquie Wood and Caroline Wilkinson for sharing needlework expertise, and Annie Warburton from the Craft Council for financial advice. I am very grateful to you all, and to my beloved family.

With special thanks to sponsors: Kitty Aldridge, Emma Freud, Isabella Tree and Charlie Burrell, Esther and Jamie Cayzer-Colvin, and Lady Jane Rayne.

For my friend and fairy godmother, Dena Hammerstein.

CHARACTERS

LADY ANNE TREE – Seventy. Upper class. No nonsense.
TOMMY – Early twenties. Londoner. On remand.
LUKASZ – Forties. Polish. Been inside eight years.
LEN – Fifties. Black. Ex-army. Lifer.
BUSBY – Thirty-five to forty-five. In a wheelchair. Repeat offender.
DERRICK/DENISE – Thirties. Back in on recall.
KEITH CLARKE – Prison officer.

The play is set in 1997 and is based on the true story of prison reform campaigner Lady Anne Tree.

This script went to press during rehearsals and may differ from the text in performance.

ACT ONE

Scene One

Six men sit on chairs. Each has a cup and a plate. They are dressed in grey tracksuit bottoms and blue T-shirts, apart from one, who is in uniform – white shirt, black trousers. As the lights come up there is a cacophony of sound, cups against plates, whistles blowing, shouts, doors slamming, feet running. Then **KEITH**, *the prison officer, stands and shouts:*

KEITH Alright everybody. Lock up. Now!

The slam of a door. Then the echo of other doors. Slam, slam, slam.

Into the silence steps **LADY ANNE TREE.** *She stands alone in a dingy, windowless room. There are a few plastic chairs and a small pool table. She has a large bag in each hand – the kind you take to the laundrette – and a key belt around her waist. She waits for a moment, and then sets the bags down. On the wall behind her is a wide flat cupboard. She checks her belt and then, remembering, takes a small key from her jacket pocket. She opens the cupboard. Inside, outlined in bright pen, are scissors, unpickers, tape measures, reels of cotton.*

Just then the overhead light goes out.

ANN Oh gawd. Hello? Hello?

The light flicks on. **BUSBY** *sits there in his wheelchair.*

BUSBY They're on a timer. Only last a few minutes. Have to press that button – the harder you press it, the longer they last.

ANNE *locks the cupboard. Puts the key back in her pocket.*

ANNE How do you do? Anne Tree.

BUSBY FF475 Busby.

ANNE Welcome, Mr Busby.

They wait.

Will it just be you?

BUSBY I'm... I think Speedy might come down if he's not on bang-up.

ANNE Right.

She unzips a bag and takes out a square of material and a skein of orange wool.

Shall we?

She pulls up a chair so that she is sitting beside **BUSBY**.

It's best to start with a simple sloping stitch – tent stitch, or half cross – not that it matters terribly what it's called. What *is* important is that the stitches all go the same way. And keeping the back tidy, that's the sign of a professional. If anything gets tangled – unpick. If it isn't perfect, we won't be able to flog it.

ANNE *has threaded the needle and now hands it to* **BUSBY** *with the material.*

Ready? So...you bring your needle up from behind, that's it, and in again above...above...and to the right, that's it, and then... Ahhh...not to worry. Slide the wool off and pull the needle through, rethread. Can you manage that?

Painstakingly he attempts to rethread. **ANNE** *offers him her glasses.*

Just the job. And start the stitch again. Now you see these little squares, change colour each square. It's rather nice if the pattern repeats, but of course, if you prefer, you can make it up as you go along.

ANNE *watches while* **BUSBY** *manages a few more stitches, frowning intently.*

BUSBY Miss, what am I making?

ANNE Oh Lord, I'm sorry. A pincushion.

She digs in her bag and finds one. A tiny brightly coloured tapestry cushion. She holds it up and, projected, it multiplies, each small cushion spinning across the back of the stage.

As the lights fade there is a jangling of keys, the rattling of metal gates, the sound of locks turning. The lights come up on:

Scene Two

TOMMY, *young, angry, scared, is being led by* **KEITH** *through the prison. He has a bedroll under his arm, and carries a cup, plate and plastic bowl. With the use of sound and light projection we see them pass through a series of holding tunnels and gates, the same locking and unlocking procedure repeated each time, until they reach the wing and a long row of cell doors.*

KEITH *stops and unlocks one.*

KEITH In you go, son, don't be shy.

Scene Three

Lights up on interior of the cell. It is lit by a fluorescent strip. There's a table, two chairs, a toilet, a basin, and a metal bunk. At the table sits **LUKASZ***, a half eaten plate of food in front of him. Behind* **TOMMY** *the door slams.*

LUKASZ The bad news – you missing tea.

He takes a mouthful, winces.

The good news – you missing tea.

He gets up and scrapes the remaining food out of the narrow slice of open window. Then from a small cupboard he takes a variety pack of cereal and a packet of UHT milk.

What will Lukasz choose today? Coco Pops. Followed by... *(He pulls out an apple.)* One fruits. You got any thing for trade? Cash. Weed. Alcohol?

TOMMY They took everything off me, didn't they? Even my fags. Get it back when I'm released, they said.

He takes a packet of Red Bull tobacco out of his pocket.

Instead I got this shit.

LUKASZ *(looks at him)* Usually I am charging double bubbles for loans. But for you, for new boy...

TOMMY Tommy.

LUKASZ For Tommy *(He takes a roll-up from behind his ear.)* you have one roll-up, then when you get funds, you pay me back, Lukasz Pietrowski, one roll-up and a half.

TOMMY You haven't got...any...

He looks around, desperate.

LUKASZ What?

TOMMY Anything to...you know...take the edge off.

LUKASZ What you think this is? A nightclub?

TOMMY I shouldn't be here.

LUKASZ I never hearing that before.

TOMMY No, it's just. I've not been sentenced.

LUKASZ Why you not get bail?

TOMMY It won't be long.

LUKASZ I can do you deal on cornflake. If was crispies I say no. But cornflake. Not my favourite.

TOMMY The lawyer, the one they gave me, he said bail might go against me, best to wait it out...

LUKASZ *(pouring milk into his cereal, eating)* So what you do then?

TOMMY What, me? Nothing.

LUKASZ Nothing? Really? Last cell mates – he never shutting up. Slicing wife from... *(draws his hand from groin to neck) pizda* to throat. He telling whole of prison. Man she was in bed with, stabbing seventeen times and...*spusic sie*...on his face.

Takes another mouthful.

TOMMY No! I just... Fucking hell!! I was drunk, that's all. I never meant... A couple of days, a week at the most, and I'll be out of here.

LUKASZ Sure, sure.

Silence.

TOMMY *(nervous)* And you? What you done then?

LUKASZ Me? Same like you. Nothing.

TOMMY How long you in for?

LUKASZ Thirteen years.

They look at each other. Lights dim and come up again on...

Scene Four

Sewing room.

ANNE *sitting with* **BUSBY.**

ANNE Marvellous. And again. That's it. Good. Ahh. Never mind. Unpick. Rethread...

She hands him glasses again.

Gently, gently... If you pull the thread too tight...

LEN *enters. A big, menacing-looking man. He coughs.* **BUSBY** *stares at his work.*

(getting up) You here for the stitching?

LEN Stitching?

The lights go out.

ANNE Blast.

There is some scrabbling. **ANNE** *gets to the switch. Lights go on.* **LEN** *and the bags are gone.*

Well, I'll be blowed.

BUSBY *carries on sewing, head down.*

LEN *(appears from behind the door)* Boo.

ANNE *(tries to recover her humour)* Ha! You nearly had me there! But seriously, any high jinks and we won't be able to get this enterprise off the ground. This is a trial, you see, and if anything goes missing they'll throw the rule book at us.

ANNE *begins laying her things out on the table.*

No wool, no kits. Especially no needles. If a needle breaks, you bring it straight to me, both ends, and I'll replace it. If you need more wool, you snip a bit off, stick it to a piece of paper, send it off, and I'll be sure to bring more in when I next come. Now.

She hands him a square of material, and a needle threaded with white wool. He stands, bemused.

Have you stitched anything before?

LEN I sewed a button on once, when I was...in the army.

ANNE An army man?

LEN Agghhhh. Pricked my bleeding finger.

ANNE No blood on that white wool!

LEN I'll do my best, Miss.

ANNE I know you will, Mr...

LEN DL476 Maxwell, Miss.

ANNE Mr Maxwell. Lady Anne Tree.

She sets a chair for him.

We're making pincushions. Ideally you use your arm to measure the length of each strand of wool, needle to elbow, then you don't get tangled up.

BUSBY What do I do when I have to cut the thread, Miss?

ANNE *uses a thread-cutter that hangs round her neck. She snips the thread for* **BUSBY**.

ANNE You're allowed nail-clippers I believe?

LUKASZ *appears in the doorway, looking through the metal bars of the gate.* **ANNE**, *sensing something, looks round but he is gone.*

LEN Or this works just as well...

He bites the wool off with his teeth.

ANNE Perhaps nail clippers might be neater? Now, start from the back, no knots, leave a tail, that's it, and bring the needle up and...down again at an angle.

LUKASZ *is at the gate again.* **ANNE** *turns.*

Will you be joining us?

LUKASZ I come to watch how you make money.

ANNE I can assure you there's no money to be made by watching.

LUKASZ *pushes open the gate and comes in.* **ANNE** *turns her attention back to* **LEN.**

Now for the next stitch, out, and down again... That's it... Do you see? Not so tight or the work becomes uneven... and again...

BUSBY *(to himself, tense)* I've messed this up.

LUKASZ *(yawning)* How long this going to take? Half hour for one tiny squares.

LEN *(quiet, threatening)* You finished my laundry yet, Busby?

BUSBY *(nervous)* I said I'd have it for you tomorrow.

ANNE *(to* **LUKASZ***)* It'll be slow at first. But you'd be surprised how one speeds up once one gets the hang of it.

LUKASZ *(flexing an arm)* I strongest man in all prison.

ANNE Sorry. I didn't get your name?

LUKASZ Pietrowski. Lukasz.

ANNE *(stands and puts out her hand)* Very nice to meet you, and congratulations, Mr Pietrowski.

They shake. The lights go out again.

Gawd!

ANNE *thumps the switch, hard. When the lights go on* **LUKASZ** *is still looking at his hand.*

Are you alright?

LUKASZ In eight years no one shook my hand.

He takes a chair and places it beside the others.

So what do I start with? Crossing stitch. Blankets stitch. Chain stitch...?

ANNE You can sew, Mr Pietrowski?

LUKASZ My mother, she was stitcher. Making clothes for whole village.

ANNE In that case, there's something here that's a little more ambitious.

Goes through her bag and draws out a kit – an image of a snarling terrier marked out on tapestry material.

Guzzle works well in cross stitch, I find. And for the collar and the...teeth...fly stitch might be awfully nice.

LUKASZ We have dog at home, on chain. Teeth? You see nothing.

ANNE *(looking at image)* He was my husband's dog.

LUKASZ Dead?

ANNE Last year, my husband. Sorry. You mean Guzzle. Very much alive.

Expertly **LUKASZ** *licks the end of his wool, twists it between his fingers and threads up. He begins to stitch, confident, flamboyant. The others look at him, daunted.*

LEN *(tangled up)* I don't think I'm cut out for this, Miss.

ANNE *(looks at his work)* It may be best to start again.

She takes it from him and begins to unpick.

You see, the work we do in here, if it's going to sell, needs to be absolutely top notch. None of this stuffed teddies, church hall nonsense. If we want it stocked in Colefax and Fowler, Liberty. Harvey Nicks!

She hands work back to **LEN.**

But let's not get ahead of ourselves. Practice makes perfect, eh? And the more you practise...

LUKASZ How long do we get? One hour in week?

ANNE We were jolly lucky to get that. But don't get me started. No. The real practice, that's what happens *between* sessions.

LUKASZ *(stops sewing)* You saying we take threads to cell?

LEN *(laughs)* Yeah? And what about my cell mate? He'll think I'm a right nancy.

ANNE *(stern)* There's nothing poofy about stitching. And you should know that, Mr Maxwell, being an army man.

LEN Army man, you're joking. After the way they washed their hands of me? Not once – and we're talking twenty years – has a single member of the armed forces lifted a finger in my defence. So don't give me army man! Jack Shit. That's what they've done for me.

He throws down his work.

Jack Shit.

ANNE Mr Maxwell, I'm so sorry.

LEN *(to* **BUSBY***)* And I want that laundry done by five. Today. You hear me? Pin cushions! What the...

LEN *thumps himself on the head and walks out.*

ANNE At least take your work with you.

But he's gone.

Mr Maxwell!

BUSBY *(holding up his sewing with a mess of orange)* Do I have to unpick this again, Miss?

ANNE *(deflated)* Yes, Mr Busby. I think you probably do.

Muted sound of phone ringing.

Scene Five

Prison wing.

TOMMY *is waiting at the payphone for someone to answer, becoming increasingly frustrated.*

TOMMY Hello, Mum? *(silence)* Hello? *(There's a little sniff.)* Lauren, is that you? It's me, Tommy... *(the sound of crying down the line)* Don't cry. Come on, girl. Where's Mum anyway? *(agitated as crying gets louder)* Mum! For Christ's sake, Lauren! *(wailing now)*

LEN *walks on and stands behind him, too close.*

Shhh, I'll be home soon... No. Not today. Not tomorrow. NO! Not cause I'm drunk. Listen. When Mum comes in, tell her I need... Lauren! I can't hear myself think.

LEN Get a shift on, son.

TOMMY *takes a slip of paper from his pocket.*

TOMMY Tell her she's got to call Mr McGarr...Garrig... *(He reads with difficulty.)* McGarrigle... He's the lawyer...the one they gave me. Can you remember that? McGarrigle. Say it back. Christ. Or tell her to go round. He never answers the fucking phone anyway... No, she can't call me. I'll try again, alright. What's that? Kelly?! What did she say? Was she...? Listen, Lauren, if you see her again... Kelly...tell her, please...

The money runs out. He looks at the phone. Fury swells.

It's a fucking joke. Two quid. For a few measly fucking minutes.

He slams the receiver against the wall. Goes to smash it, but **LEN** *grabs him from behind, and is about to lay into him when he stops himself. He holds him very still.*

LEN Twat.

He picks up the receiver. He shakes it. It's still working.

It's your lucky day, mate.

He lets go of **TOMMY**, *puts his card in and dials. The phone is picked up almost immediately.*

Hello, darling... Yeah, and you.

TOMMY *slumps against the wall.*

So, what you up to? Blimey. Sounds a bit exerting. You want to be careful. Too right. Make yourself comfortable, why don't you. You're slipping off your shoes... Good girl, why don't I give your feet a rub? Feels good eh? And while you're at it, might as well slip out of...

He looks round at **TOMMY**.

Are you going to fuck off or what?

TOMMY *slopes off.* **LEN** *turns back to phone.*

Oh you have, have you? For me? Better slide that off and all. Slowly now. Mmmm, lovely darling, What's that? Who's calling round at this time? Ignore it. Ignore it, I said. I couldn't give a toss if it's... Tell her to bleeding... Trish...? Trisha!

He puts his head in his hands. Moans.

BUSBY *rolls on in his wheelchair.*

And, Busby, you can fuck off an' all.

BUSBY *spins round and wheels off again.*

Bitch.

He slams down the receiver.

Scene Six

Prison cell.

TOMMY *lies on the bottom bunk. He's really suffering now. DTs. On the floor beside him* LUKASZ *is doing press-ups. Two-armed. One-armed. Up against the wall. He counts in Polish.*

LUKASZ *Szesnascie, siebemnascie, osiemnascie, dziewietnascie,* twenty!

He stands and stretches.

Now you.

TOMMY I'm alright thanks, Poland.

LUKASZ When I first inside I was weakling. Much trouble. Now I am strong, not so much.

TOMMY *rolls off his bunk, and starts doing half-hearted press-ups.* LUKASZ *stands over him.*

I do one for wife. Up. One for children. Up. One for mother. Hup. None for father. Down. Down. He bastard. One for barscht. One for vodka. One for pickles mother make in autumn. Red pepper. Aubergine. One more for pancake. Butter. Charlotka. Plum.

TOMMY *(lying flat on the floor)* I do one for bit of fucking quiet.

LUKASZ How ever long or short you in here, you need must look strong. Yes? If not look strong you, how you say...fucked.

TOMMY *jumps up and starts kicking the wall.*

TOMMY I'm already fucked. You hear that?

LUKASZ Relax. Boxing is good too.

He punches imaginary punch bag.

You do one for Lukasz. Strongest man in prison. Maybe more than one. Maybe hundred.

TOMMY *punches imaginary bag.*

Maybe one for girlfriend?

TOMMY Just give it a rest, why don't you.

He rakes fingers through hair, winces in pain.

LUKASZ How much you drinking, on the out?

TOMMY Who's counting?

LUKASZ Ha! So is your girl who wanting you inside.

TOMMY Just leave it will you. Or...find me something. Don't they brew their own in here?

LUKASZ Sure. I get you for two phonecard. You want hooch? They make with metal polish, store in fire extinguisher.

Stands very still before him.

Or easier, I kick you in the head?

There is a loud banging on the wall and a shout.

VOICE Burglar!

LUKASZ We got three and a half minutes.

LUKASZ *opens drawers, jams phonecards and several bags of tobacco under his shirt.* **TOMMY** *straightens up his bed. While he does this,* **LUKASZ** *slips a homemade knife from under his pillow and, unseen by* **TOMMY**, *goes to the window, stands on a chair, pulls in a string, ties it to the handle and drops the knife out. There is the sound of a bottle smashing.* **TOMMY** *runs to the window, squeezes onto the chair, looks out.*

TOMMY Fuck!

Another bottle smashes.

How does something that size get smuggled in?

LUKASZ You be amazed what fit up there.

There is a thump on the door. The sound of a dog barking.

TOMMY What a fucking waste.

KEITH *(voice)* Cell search.

LUKASZ *bangs on the other wall.*

LUKASZ Burglar! Now *they* got three and a half minutes.

The door is opened.

KEITH Alright. You two. Out!

KEITH *searches the cell. Finds nothing.*

Bastard.

Scene Seven

ANNE'*s house.*

Birdsong. Chintz armchair. Framed cross stitch portrait of a terrier – Guzzle. There is a desk with a typewriter and dial-up telephone beside a stack of floral diaries.

ANNE, *flustered, is typing with two fingers.*

ANNE I am writing to you in the hope of eliciting support for a charity I am most anxious to get off the ground.

She pulls out paper. Rolls another one in.

Even in my earliest days, and I have been involved in prison work since 1952, it was all too apparent...

Another piece of paper.

I do recognise that it has been against prison policy for convicts to earn money, aside from the most basic prison pay, but now, with this welcome change in the law, and with the Royal School of Needlework willing to get involved...

More paper.

Cushions, quilts, immensely saleable, mail order, and with a large percentage of the purchase price going to the stitcher... I feel optimistic that this scheme...

ANNE *looks up and out.*

I look forward, very much, to hearing your response.

Scene Eight

Prison cell.

TOMMY *is sitting on the toilet. His head and shoulders visible above a small curtain.* **LUKASZ** *enters.*

TOMMY Poland. Mate!

LUKASZ What you want, I knock?

He wafts air with his hand.

When I first inside we have bucket. Three men, shit and piss. Slop out one time a day.

TOMMY *(flushing)* You've been gone hours!

LUKASZ Enhance Thinking Skill.

TOMMY You what?

LUKASZ *(parrot fashion)* A new approach to think and work out problem. With aim to reduce reoffend behaviour.

TOMMY Let *me* out. I'll prove it works.

LUKASZ Is a course to help imagine other people feelings.

TOMMY All I know is...there's going to be trouble if I don't get out of...

LUKASZ You on remand, what you expect?

TOMMY ...out of...this fucking cell.

LUKASZ When you get sentence, then you get plan. Then, like me, you spend happy afternoon to find right answer: "Is long while since you have visit and you look forward very much, but person not arrive..." Do you: One. Fly in rage. Two. Call to insults them. Or three – consider something not in their controls happening to stop visit?"

TOMMY I'd call to have a go at them if it wasn't going to bankrupt me. What's the story with the phones in here? They cost ten times what they do outside. It'll take more than a course in enhanced fucking thinking to get my head round that one.

LUKASZ Soap – luxury. Deodorant – luxury. Talk to outside... for luxury you pay.

TOMMY My mum, she was in earlier, with my kid sister... Says she'll come again, but what's the... Fucking useless. If my dad was here... Next time, I'll say no. No visits. The guard, he had to drag her off me, didn't he? Lauren. What I wouldn't have done to him... The cunt...I'm telling you, I'd be in here forever.

Needs to distract himself.

What else they teach you then?

LUKASZ We is learning: Define Problem.

TOMMY What the fuck.

LUKASZ A problem is gap...between you are...and you want to be. So...you want to go to pub, but no money. Problem is gap. Pub – no money. Gap. You understand?

TOMMY *looks at him blankly.*

(holds up his hands) Me same. Then we is using CAF – *(He reads writing on hand.)* consider all factor. FIP – first important priority *(He looks at his other hand.)* and PMI – plus minus interesting bit. And still, all I understand is I is problem. That is only thing I understand.

TOMMY No. *This* is the problem.

He kicks the walls.

Twenty-three-hour fucking bang-up. And Kelly...she's in the hospital, complications, my mum said, from when she... When she fell... *(struggles to control himself)* And there's... Can't even buy her a sodding bunch of flowers.

He jumps onto the chair and puts his face to the slice of open window.

Let me out! Help me! Yes. You down there. You nosy fuck. Ten minutes. That's all I ask. Ten minutes.

TOMMY *slides down the wall.*

I can't handle this, man. I shouldn't be here.

LUKASZ *climbs onto his bed, he lifts up his pillow and takes out his embroidery, quietly humming as he sews. The room slowly darkens. A low keening sound fills the space – it is coming from the segregation block. Soon it turns to howls, echoing around the prison, and then other men's voices can be heard.*

PRISONER 1 Shut the fuck up, you fraggle.

PRISONER 2 Quiet, you nutter.

PRISONER 1 I'll fucking gut you. Want that, do you?

The howls continue. **LUKASZ** *lies down and puts the pillow over his head.* **TOMMY**, *still huddled against the wall, puts his hands over his ears. The volume of noise rises – shouts and screams of abuse. Banging and drumming. There's a blast of music – hip-hop with a shattering base. A crash. Then someone starts to sing – "**JOLENE**" by Dolly Parton. A lone voice but it cuts through.*

PRISONER *sings first verse of* "***JOLENE***".

Other **PRISONERS** *join in. Then, on the second verse,* **LUKASZ** *sings too.*

Slowly the lights go up, and the singing is overtaken by the sound of a prison officer stamping along the corridor:

KEITH *(chanting)* The Chelsea boys, we are here, To fuck your women and drink your beer.

The sound of cell doors unlocking.

Breakfast. Now.

Voices and feet on the metal stairways. A sharp whistle. Silence.

Scene Nine

Sewing room.

ANNE *sits at the table. She lays out her different coloured wool, marking her supplies on a sheet of paper.*

ANNE Maroon. Burnt umber. Aquamarine. Cinnamon. Tangerine.

ANNE *looks up regularly. Nothing. Then* **KEITH** *puts his head round the door.*

KEITH You won't be seeing anyone today.

ANNE Don't tell me. No free flow.

KEITH Half the officers out at a funeral.

ANNE Sorry to hear that.

KEITH Heart attack. Young fellow. Only been working here six months.

ANNE And sorry for the men too – banged up till tomorrow.

KEITH They should have thought of that before they broke the law.

They look at each other.

Right. You want an escort? I'll see you out.

ANNE Thank you, but that shan't be necessary.

She clanks the keys on her belt.

KEITH If you're not gone by four-thirty, you'll have to bunk up here, and you won't be popular. There's some of them already three to a cell.

KEITH *exits. We see* **ANNE** *packing up her bag and walking out along the wing.*

Scene Ten

ANNE *stops before the row of closed doors. She approaches one and looking round and, seeing no one, she opens the flap. Quickly she flips it shut again.*

ANNE Terribly sorry. Excuse me.

ANNE *moves to the next door and taps on it with her keys.*

Hello? Are you decent?

She gets a positive reply and opens the flap.

I know this might sound a bit off the wall, but I wanted to let you know about a project I'm setting up. Stitching. A chance to learn a skill and earn a bit of money while you're at it. Really? A nest egg for when you get out? Have a think. I know it's unusual, but... Very well.

ANNE *moves along to the next cell and taps on the door.*

Hello?

She opens the flap.

Ah, Mr Maxwell, I rather hoped I might find you. No. I do understand. It's just I had a feeling, a sort of hunch that you might be the right sort for my scheme. My father was an army man you see, said it was the saving of them, the POWs, when they got hold of a bit of sewing. Something to make, mend even.... In that case, I apologise. I won't take up any more of your time.... Sorry? The first war, my brother fought in the second. Coldstream Guards. Armoured division. Nearly made it too. What's that? Tuesday. Yes. Every week.

Scene Eleven

Prison cell.

A light flashes, pulsing red across the stage. **KEITH** *lifts the flap.*

KEITH Now what's the problem?

TOMMY What's the problem? Are you serious? I've got to get out. I need a break.

KEITH What were you thinking...Honolulu or the Isle of Wight?

TOMMY Just anywhere...outside. The yard would do.

KEITH Sorry mate. And if you press that button again you'll get a nicking. If you press it three times you'll be up before the Governor. Then you'll be in trouble.

TOMMY I'm in trouble now.

KEITH *(softens)* Soon as you know what you're doing, you can put an app in for some classes. Shouldn't be too long.

TOMMY Shouldn't be too long. What does that mean?

KEITH A few months maybe? Never much more than a year.

TOMMY A year?!

Kicks the door.

But I haven't been sentenced! I haven't even got a date.

KEITH While you're on this wing, you'll not be judged for what you've done outside, alright? You'll be judged for how you behave in here. I always say, I don't care if they're mass murderers, they spit at an officer... Don't be pressing that button again.

KEITH *bangs the flap shut.* **TOMMY** *stands still.*

TOMMY She lost the baby, didn't she. Kelly. And I can't even say I'm sorry.

TOMMY *runs on the spot, faster and faster and then defeated, more slowly.*

Scene Twelve

Sewing room.

LUKASZ *stands before* **ANNE** *with his work.*

LUKASZ Is just me today, Miss. Big trouble on D wing. Lockdown since Monday.

ANNE Very well.

LUKASZ Cheese Barron attacking Busby.

ANNE Oh dear.

LUKASZ Then man, quiet man, usually quiet man, taking two men hostage. He use scissors for trapping them in cell. *(instinctively she puts her hand to her pocket)* Shouting for Governor, three hours, for hearing his demands.

ANNE What were his demands?

LUKASZ He free for move to open prison, near to home. Four months, no one available for drive him.

ANNE Mr Pietrowski, and how have you been getting on?

LUKASZ *(holding out embroidery for her inspection)* Last week I starting to stitch, before I know, they open door for breakfast. Is addictive, like drug. Then I running out of wool.

ANNE *(taking his work)* Stick a sample to an envelope and send it off! What did I say?

Looks for wool.

LUKASZ Watch for slip under door, they tell him, and in the morning you be move. He watch, he wait, but slip never come.

ANNE Basket stitch. Is that a stitch you know?

LUKASZ He patient, he patient...then...snap. Now they putting him in seg.

They hear a distant howl of anguish.

ANNE *(very focused)* You stitch down lengths of string in parallel lines, with the distance between not less than the width of the string.

LEN *strides in carrying his embroidery.*

LEN Sorry I'm late.

They both look at him, startled.

Didn't think I was ever getting out. Can't trust any one in here.

ANNE You knew the man?

LEN I know him a whole lot better now.

ANNE You were the hostage?

LEN Three hours! Fingers got a bit wobbly when he held the scissors to my throat, but I got on with my stitching.

Holds it out.

'Fraid I made a pig's ear of some of it.

ANNE *inspects.*

ANNE You have rather.

LEN *slumps in a chair.*

LEN Missed a stitch when he threw the scissors out the window.

ANNE What are we waiting for? *(jokingly forceful)* Unpick!

LUKASZ Ahh, that's what I missing...soft voice of woman.

LEN *(starts unpickng)* A decent shower. That's what I miss. Why are the showers on the spur stone cold? And if you go up to the threes, you get scalded. When I complain, what did the Gov say: "What? With your thick hide?"

LUKASZ I offering to sort it out. I know good plumber! But they not allow that. Afraid I attack someone with spanner.

BUSBY *wheels in, his head is wrapped in a bandage. He comes forward to show his work.*

ANNE Mr Busby.

Takes work.

Are you alright under there?

BUSBY *flinches, but doesn't answer.*

You've got an extra stitch, just here, it's jumbling it all up. Best do that square again.

BUSBY *nods, gets on with his work.*

LUKASZ Cheese Baron, he pour sugar in kettle, then when water boil... *(mimes throwing)* sugar melt in skin.

LEN Why you do it, Busby. *(to the others)* Filched a letter, didn't he, stupid c... *(stops himself, coughs)* Can't help himself. In and out of this place like a bloody yoyo. Last time, two weeks was it you were gone? Wheeling down the road, minding his own business, passed a house with the keys in the front door!

BUSBY *(head down, sewing)* Unlucky.

LUKASZ You hear Cheese Barron attacking Speedy and all. Say he snitch on him for stashing milk supply.

ANNE *moves to the light and pushes it on.*

LEN It wasn't Speedy. I can vouch for that. He was out there in the yard, running a marathon with me.

ANNE A marathon?

LEN Ran seven miles last week. For lung cancer. Well, not *for* lung cancer. For a cure. My wife...she...she's in remission now but... Five times round is one mile.

ANNE And Speedy?

LUKASZ Probably in cell now, running up walls.

BUSBY *(wheels himself closer to* **ANNE**. *Low voice)* What will I do, if I get stuck again, Miss. Before next week, I mean.

ANNE *looks across at* **LUKASZ.**

ANNE You'll help Mr Busby, won't you? If he needs guidance.

LUKASZ I not have time.

ANNE Come on!

LUKASZ I not know how to find him.

ANNE You could check on him, surely. During Association. See how he's getting on.

LUKASZ *(reluctant)* What cell you in?

BUSBY C1-07.

LUKASZ C1-07?! I use be in that cell.

BUSBY Really?

LUKASZ Two years! I know C1-07. I call on you. Tomorrow.

BUSBY I'll be there.

ANNE I had a threader here somewhere, and now I can't find it.

They all look down at their work.

Where is the blasted thing?

A woman – **DENISE** *– stands at the gate. She has false eyelashes, make-up. Styled hair. Otherwise dressed in usual prison garb.*

LEN Derrick?

DENISE Is there room for a small one?

LEN What you done to yourself? What you doing back here?

DENISE Missed you too much, Len.

LEN *(tense)* Give over.

DENISE Late for my probation officer. Five minutes. Well, fifteen. What's a girl to do, my nail's weren't dry. Back on recall.

ANNE Do you sew, Mr umm..

DENISE Whatever they can do I can do better.

DENISE *goes to inspect each man's work. First* **BUSBY**.

Shame.

Then **LEN**.

Never mind, darling.

Then **LUKASZ**.

Who's a clever boy? *(admiring Guzzle)* This your little pet?

ANNE Guzzle. My husband. I mean, my husband's dog. Nothing but trouble, if I'm honest. But irresistible all the same.

DENISE Sounds like someone else I know.

LEN I'm warning you!

ANNE *rummages in her bag.*

ANNE A lavender bag might be nice to start with. Sorry, I didn't catch your name?

DENISE Denise.

ANNE *(checks paperwork)* Not sure you're on the list... Have you had clearance?

DENISE A4792H. It'll be a mix-up, that's all. Officially I've been discharged. I've done my time. Haven't I served my time?

LUKASZ Derrick done his time. I not know about Denise.

DENISE I'll make a start, and then I'll hand it over when I say my goodbyes. You can finish it for me. Can't you, darling?

LEN You do your own lavender bag. Alright?

DENISE Prickly.

ANNE Choose a colour.

She holds out a wheel of threads.

DENISE So many! Just one?

Closes eyes. Picks.

Scarlet!

Lights dim and come up on:

Scene Thirteen

We hear a muted phone ringing.

LEN, LUKASZ *and* **DENISE** *are lit by the light of a TV screen. They are watching "Shawshank Redemption". We see the final scenes of the film projected onto the wall.*

Scene Fourteen

TOMMY *is on the phone.*

TOMMY Is she with you? My mum? Yeah, yeah, Happy Christmas to you too, Nan. *(A rat runs by, he starts back)* Where's she got to? Don't tell me...not with him. So where's Lauren then?

The last scene of "Shawshank Redemption" rolls. Morgan Freeman and Tim Robbins are on the screen, free men, meeting and embracing by the blue Pacific. The final credits run.

DENISE I love a bit of hope, but it can drive you insane.

LEN And I should know. Another year nearly gone. Another appeal waiting to be heard.

LUKASZ That is fifth time I see Shawshank, and I still sure Red getting parole before forty years pass by. It hurt me, every time.

LEN You heard about the old guy in D wing? He had so many knock-backs doesn't want to be considered any more. Close my file, he said. I'm giving up.

DENISE Maybe I could get hold of a Rita Hayworth poster for you, Len, then you can tunnel your way out too.

LEN *(affronted)* I'll be leaving here with my head held high thank you very much, Derrick! Publicly exonerated. My wife waiting by the gate with flowers. My grandkids... *(He is interrupted by the sound of horns and trumpets.)* Bloody hell!

Projected, we see a Salvation Army Band. God Rest You Merry Gentlemen morphs into Silent Night.

DENISE No homes to go to, on Christmas and all, poor loves.

LEN For a minute I thought it was a holy fucking chorus come to tell me – yes, we believe you. You never done it. We're here to set you free.

TOMMY *(replaces phone and joins them. Quiet)* Poland, mate. Lend us another phonecard, will you. I've got to...got to try and get a message to...to Kelly.

LUKASZ What about your job. You not get paid?

TOMMY Seven quid for a week of cleaning floors...

LUKASZ *(miming stitching)* While you sit doing nothing I earning twenty quids.

TOMMY I said I'll pay you back!

LUKASZ *(pulling out phonecard)* What about the other times you promising to pay me back. You no new kid now.

TOMMY Double bubble. I swear it.

The Salvation Army continue to play, but more quietly as if they have moved away. **TOMMY** *goes to the phone. He dials and waits. It rings and rings, then finally someone answers, but doesn't speak.*

Hello? Lauren? Is that you? Is Mum there?

The sound of crying comes down the line. **TOMMY** *closes his eyes.*

Listen. Listen to me...

The whimpers subside.

It's alright. She'll be back, she always comes back, remember? That's it. Shhh... What's that? I wanted to... But there's not much... I haven't...

He looks around. Then he turns his back on the men.

Here's something alright? *(begins to sing very quietly into the phone Elton John's "**YOUR SONG**" changing the word "boy" to "girl")*

LEN *looks over at* **TOMMY**.

LEN The kid's never off the fucking phone!

TOMMY *still singing.*

LEN *walks over and stands very close.*

LEN Come on man, time's up.

TOMMY *sings the last line of the second verse.*

LEN *(pokes him on the shoulder)* Are you deaf or what?

TOMMY *(defiantly sings the first line of the third verse at* **LEN**, *then goes back to Lauren)* Listen, Lauren, when Mum comes in, tell her to... I need her to get hold of Kelly... Tell her to go round...

LEN What do you think it is...?

TOMMY After dark then...

LEN ...Christmas?

TOMMY *drops the phone, and with a roar he throws himself at* **LEN**, *pummelling and thrashing at him.* **DENISE** *shrieks and attempts to shield* **LEN**, *who shakes her off.* **TOMMY** *gets a punch in before* **LUKASZ** *pulls him away.* **TOMMY** *struggles to free himself but* **LUKASZ** *holds him down, taking the next blow, and then unable to restrain himself he launches himself at* **LEN**. *As the Salvation Army music builds to a crescendo,* **TOMMY** *leaps up and* **BUSBY**, *his embroidery in his lap, wheels into the fray. A whistle blows.*

Scene Fifteen

ANNE*'s house.*

The sound of birdsong. She is going over a speech.

ANNE Initially, a couple of hundred or more years ago, prison was solely the place in which a person was confined while awaiting trial. No one had the idea that prison itself was a successful punishment.

There is a ferocious barking offstage.

Guzzle! Stop that. Ahh, Jenkins, thank you, no need to come closer, do leave the post there. Guzzle! Honestly!

ANNE *turns to the front, still practising.*

I was a very young woman when I first became a prison visitor. In my day a private word from someone in the know was what it took. Diana Mosley vouched for me. She was locked up, as was her husband, beastly man, the fascist, Oswald, for their own good, during the war. I had to visit. Her sister Debo was married to my brother. It was then that I saw how many people had no visitors at all.

ANNE *checks her speech.*

(talking to herself) Will they grill me about Myra, I wonder? People are ghoulish.

Makes a note.

Especially in the WI.

Back to speech.

Where was I? Yes. For generations the habit of incarcerating people went unquestioned. Conditions were dreadful. People lived like beasts. Then the Quakers got involved. They visited prisons, treated convicts as human beings, with souls, but they did nothing to lift the veil of secrecy in which prison still exists.

Scene Sixteen

Sewing room.

The sewing cupboard is open. One pair of scissors gone. **ANNE** *uses them to cut squares from a sample book of Colefax and Fowler chintz.*

BUSBY *has improved hugely. He's working on the background of two artichokes.* **LEN** *is still embroidering something simple – a needle case.* **LUKASZ**, *the expert, has moved onto a quilt. Many chintz squares are spread out before him.* **DENISE** *is absent.*

LUKASZ Sorry I not get to class last week, Lady Anne. No one free for unlocking me.

ANNE Again! I'm sorry too. But I like to think of it as more of a club than a class. And no Mr... Denise? Dare I assume... he...she has been released?

LUKASZ Five days he not get out of bed. Headache he saying but...

ANNE Well at least she can see the lavender bags...

ANNE *lifts a finished lavender bag out of her bag, and then another and another. Six in all. She places them on the table.*

...which really do look rather fine. Although, Mr Busby, I have to say, I'm staggered at your progress with those artichokes. Not an easy design by any means, I've stitched a few myself.

LEN *(to* **LUKASZ***)* Cheese Baron tried to get in on the action, did you hear? Came along all pally as can be. But I warned you, didn't I? He's trouble. There was a rumour on the spur he was planning to get Busby to do the stitching for him, get hold of a kit, farm it out, get hold of another one, but it's not how it works, isn't that right?

ANNE *smiles at* **LEN**.

You should have seen him then. Turned nasty. Had to be hauled out. Lady Anne, could you take a shufti at my needle case?

LUKASZ If he causing more trouble, we throw him round like rag doll, yes boys?

LEN Leave it to us. We'll sort him.

LUKASZ We taking pool ball and we smashing...

LEN We'll serve him up. Right lads?

ANNE Thank you. I'm sure that won't be necessary.

ANNE *looks around, apprehensive.*

(handing back needlecase.) That's very nice. Change colour maybe?

LEN Getting nastier, have you noticed, since they confiscated his iron.

ANNE His iron?

LEN Ran a racket from his cell. Couple packets sliced white. Cheese filched from the kitchen. *(mimes pressing down with an iron)* Toasties!

LUKASZ In Poland cheese ninety per cent cheese, in here cheese ten per cent cheese.

TOMMY *appears at the door.*

TOMMY *(nervous)* Is this the sewing class?

LEN *(in posh accent)* We like to think of it as more of a club.

Laughter. **TOMMY** *comes in, tentatively.*

TOMMY GH6732, Miss.

ANNE Anne.

TOMMY Tommy.

ANNE Welcome, Tommy.

She has finished with the scissors and replaces them in the cubooard. She locks it after her and puts the key in her pocket.

Let's find something to start you off.

She sets a chair for him beside her. Pulls out a kit.

A butterfly, I think.

BUSBY *wheels over to the light switch and punches it on.*

BUSBY Got you.

ANNE Marvellous. That's three in a row you've got the better of.

TOMMY *(staring at the square of material)* I don't know... I'm not sure.

ANNE *measures length of wool, hand to elbow, snips it.*

ANNE You'll want to divide your thread. Lasts longer and it's easier to manage. Very slowly. Too fast and it gets tangled. There. Now, hold the threat tight, close to the end, and push it through the eye of the needle, or lick it.

He manages this. Ties a knot.

No knots! No, no. Snip that off.

She snips it.

We want to keep the back tidy. Now. We'll start with running stitch. In through the back, leaving a tail, then down again, and up, the same distance apart. Down and up. Ah. You want the stitches the same size. Don't worry. Keep going.

She watches.

You see, that stitch was neater, so...progress. Keep it on the line. On the line...

TOMMY *is becoming flustered.*

It's alright. Anything worth doing... You see, perfection is not usually expected of prisoners *(looking round)* but we're going to show them, aren't we, gentlemen?

She waits.

That's it. Terrific. So. Back stitch. Ready? Push the needle into the end of the last stitch, and out. Good job! Ahh, your thread's caught up. Not to worry. You'll have to pull the needle off and rethread. You do that and we'll have a go at chain.

TOMMY *(panicking, struggling to thread)* It won't go.

LEN Don't be daft. You could get a camel through that.

ANNE Threader. Hmm. Disappeared again.

LUKASZ In here? Who you think we are?

TOMMY *has succeeded in threading the needle.*

TOMMY Done it!

ANNE Jolly good. So. You work chain from the top of the line, down towards you. Much like running stitch but you make a loop...

A rat scuttles across the back of the room. **TOMMY** *looks round as it disappears through a hole, but everyone else is so engrossed in their work that they don't notice.*

Insert needle, careful not to twist it, the loop should lie flat and form a rounded shape.

TOMMY Bring needle up at the top?

ANNE Yes...

TOMMY Insert needle...

LUKASZ Same position.

ANNE That's it, down again. And bring it up a *short* distance... If the stitch is too long it will look spidery...

LEN We don't want that!

TOMMY And pull the needle through.

ANNE That's it. Excellent.

TOMMY Insert...needle...

BUSBY *(suddenly angry, thumping with his wheelchair)* Miss Anne, there's a real problem here.

He tips up the front wheels and slams them down.

ANNE Oh Lord, what is it?

BUSBY There's a real problem, and it's not going to go away.

The tension in the room is palpable.

This cream wool is not the same shade as the cream wool that I've been using!

ANNE *Can* that be the case?

She inspects it.

Oh... How maddening! But...I sent the batch number to the manufacturers and this is what they sent back.

BUSBY I've put a hundred hours at least into these two artichokes. And now the background's all messed up.

BUSBY *wheels away and slams his chair into the door. Then he swings round. He looks as if he is going to run them all down.* **ANNE** *stands her ground.* **BUSBY** *takes a deep breath, bangs his fist against the light switch.*

I'll unpick it. If it's going to be perfect, there's nothing else for it.

ANNE Good man.

BUSBY It's not like I've got anything else pressing to do.

The men all sew. **ANNE** *checks on their progress.*

ANNE *(frowning down at* **TOMMY***'s effort)* Spidery, do you see. We want it nice and round.

She waits.

That's it. Better.

She flicks through the pile of squares.

(to **LUKASZ***)* Can I interest you in any more Honeysuckle Chintz?

LUKASZ *(looking at his arrangement. Reading labels on the back)* You have more Garden Party? And yes. Plumbago Bouquet.

LEN Plumbago. I think my Gran suffered from that.

DENISE*, pale, dishevelled, appears in the doorway.*

DENISE What have I missed?

ANNE *(holds up lavender bags)* Stuffed! The lot of them.

DENISE I'd make a joke, but I'm... I'm not...

ANNE Start something new?

ANNE *holds up a kit for a cushion with a heart and an arrow going through it.*

DENISE That'll take forever... Oh yeah. Go on then.

Pause as they all sew.

LUKASZ When you first come inside, Lady Anne?

LEN Yeah. How much time you served?

ANNE I became a prison visitor...it must be... I had a...a relative in Holloway, during the war.

LEN Rough place I heard, Holloway.

DENISE I asked to be sent there...

LUKASZ What they doing? Murder?

LEN Fraud. That's what the rich ones are in for. Everything else they get away with.

LUKASZ You stitching with them?

ANNE A friend of my husband inherited a really magnificent Aubusson rug. An antique. Beautiful, huge, but falling apart. We were looking it over, talking about having it copied, and he happened to say, the problem is, it would take so much time. And that's when it struck me. I knew people with time. We set up in a special room. You've never seen anything more ravishing. They took such care. And when it was finished it was valued at ten thousand pounds. I went to the Governor of Holloway and asked if an account could be set up for the women, and some money paid into it. The money they were owed. It could be given to their families, or saved for them when they got out. But no. That was against the law. And if I were to collect the money, and hand it over surreptitiously? I'd most probably end up in Holloway myself.

LUKASZ Who is making that law?

ANNE How to reverse it. That was the challenge.

BUSBY When I was last released, they gave me thirty-seven quid, and told me I'd have my first dole cheque in six weeks. I went to my ma's. She was still alive then, but I couldn't stick it. Not with a...certain person living next door. If I could have just gone down to the local for a pint, or bought something to make my ma a meal. Maybe if it had of been summer...but the winter days in... I never saw that dole cheque, I don't know if it arrived, I was already back inside by then. *(starts scratching his hands)* There's something worrying me. Once this is unpicked, what am I to do until the right shade of cream arrives?

LEN Ahh, bloody hell I just stitched my trouser legs together. The shock of Busby talking. Been on the same spur five years...

ANNE *looks through her bag.*

ANNE I'm afraid it's back to pincushions. A bit of a comedown I know...

She keeps searching.

Wait, I do have something. You're probably not going to want to hear this, but there's a kit here for *three* artichokes.

BUSBY You're bloody joking! *(takes a moment)* Go on then. Hand it over.

The lights go out.

LUKASZ See. You start talking. You forgetting your job.

BUSBY Alright. I'm on my way.

He wheels towards the light switch, as the lights go on, **TOMMY** *is stuffing wool into his pocket.* **ANNE** *turns to him, he looks up at her, alarmed.*

ANNE How are you getting on, Tommy? Ahh. Let me show you again.

She takes the work.

Do you see how these have got a bit bunched together?

TOMMY I've messed it up.

ANNE Not at all.

TOMMY I'm rubbish...

ANNE We all mess up, Tommy. The key is not to mind too much when you have to start again. Bring your needle up from underneath, curl your thread round...

LUKASZ Don't be getting to rely on this boy, Lady Anne, he on remand, from one day to next he gone.

ANNE Do you have a date then? For your hearing?

TOMMY I did have. But I had to let the lawyer go... He was a... We didn't... Now I don't know what's going on.

ANNE *puts her hand on his shoulder.*

DENISE It's the not knowing, that's what's hard.

LEN And the knowing. I got news today. They turned down my appeal.

Pause.

ANNE When I was a girl, my mother took my sister and me to the Old Bailey. We sat through a whole trial. We didn't have school – in our family, school for girls was considered wrong-headed – so maybe it was a chance to broaden our "non-education." After three long weeks, the verdict came back: guilty. Although it didn't seem at all clear to me that was the case. But what did I know? I was only ten.

LUKASZ Your sister, she a prison visitor too?

ANNE She became a Justice of the Peace.

LEN She sends them down, you cheer them back up.

ANNE I hadn't thought of that. Mr Maxwell, might this be a good time to teach you how to make a French knot?

Lights down. Noise of the prison rising up like a wave.

Scene Seventeen

We see **KEITH** *walking along the wing, unlocking cell doors. Then walking back, slamming them shut.*

The rain comes pouring down.

Scene Eighteen

ANNE *with an umbrella. She is calling her dog.*

ANNE Guzzle. Guzzle. Guuuuuuuzle.

She walks back and forth, calling and waiting and calling again.

Blast it! Where are you?

Hand in pocket.

Biscuits.

Scene Nineteen

Prison cell.

TOMMY *is sitting at the small table with a schoolwork sheet and a pen. He reads, with difficulty.* **LUKASZ** *is hanging strands of wool on nails in the wall.*

TOMMY "What collar...colour...shirt is the boy wea...ring." How the fuck should I know.

Sighs, frowns, goes back to the beginning of the paper he is reading from.

"The boy wal...walked down the road. It was hot and his... shoes drudge, dragged. He...he...oh fuck it... What colour would his shirt be? White? Blue, chances are.

He writes laboriously.

B le oooo.

LUKASZ *starts to hum.*

Cut it out, will you.

LUKASZ You try making stitch. Is good for calm.

TOMMY I tried it. Alright. I'm rubbish.

He continues reading.

The boys shoes drudged, dragged, and the sun sh... What did the boy's shoes...

He gives up.

Fucking rubbish.

The men sit in silence. **LUKASZ** *begins to sing, putting words to the Polish song that he's been humming.*

LUKASZ

SŁONECZKO ZASZŁO, CZYLI ZAGASŁO,
I JUZ SIE SCIEMNIA, PRZED WIECZOREM.

TOMMY *picks up his pen and starts drawing on the wall. Four bars and a fifth slashing through them. One month. Then another month. Then another. He rests his head against the wall.* **KEITH** *walks along the corridor, unlocking the cells. The jangle of keys.*

I read one time there is no past, no future, there is only now.

TOMMY *looks at him in disbelief.*

TOMMY Are you having me on?

LEN *pushes open the door, sewing in his hand.*

LEN Sorry to disturb, but do you, have you got...any pink wool?

LUKASZ What is worth to you?

LEN It's the French knots. The pattern repeats and I'm short a few strands... I'll give you some maroon?

LUKASZ Aquamarines?

LEN Tricky. I can part with a bit of... *(pulls thread out of pocket, looks at label)* burnt umber?

LUKASZ *puts out his hand.* **LEN** *passes over wool.* **LUKASZ** *takes a strand of pink off the wall. The two men nod at each other.*

TOMMY What do you think to this, Len? Poland here is suggesting there's no such thing as time.

LUKASZ Just *now*. No past, no future.

LEN All I know is that whether you think about it or not, however you count it, or not, it passes. That's all I've learnt.

TOMMY When I came in last summer Wimbledon was on, and I thought to myself, what if I'm still inside next Wimbledon. What if I'm still here then? I couldn't get it out of my head.

LUKASZ For me is Christmas. One Christmas, tick, two Christmas, tick, eight Christmas...

TOMMY Sorry, I know the time I've been in here – it's nothing compared...

LUKASZ One Wimbledon, next Wimbledon, still long time.

LEN Not too long now till the World Cup.

TOMMY World Cup. In here. That's just...wrong.

He looks at **LEN**.

If you don't mind me asking, Len, how many World Cups you been inside for?

LEN It's wedding anniversaries for me. We got married in September. Me and Trish. Rained. Meant to be lucky! But World Cups. That's... Bloody hell... There's this one coming up right... High hopes for Beckham, no? But let's see... '94, first ever final to be won on pens. Before that... '90. Gazza blubbed, and before that... Ha! The hand of God scored a goal for Argentina.

TOMMY Maradona?

LEN That's it.

TOMMY I was just a little kid.

LEN And before that...

TOMMY No!

LEN There was that semi-final with West Germany beating France on pens. One of the best World Cup matches of all time. I was in Pentonville. Lodging my first appeal. Still thought I had a chance. Thought someone would listen.

TOMMY So all my life, even when my dad was around, watching those games, bunking off school, getting into trouble. Ibiza! Kelly. All that time you've been inside?

LEN Don't worry about it, son. If I could admit to being guilty, I'd have been a free man years ago.

TOMMY Bloody hell.

LUKASZ Wimbledon. World Cup. Inside. Outside. We all doing time.

LEN *(holding up pink wool)* Cheers mate. Appreciate it.

Scene Twenty

ANNE*'s house.*

ANNE *is making a telephone call.*

ANNE The Governor. Thank you. *(waits)* Ahh, hello. Yes. I'd like to speak to Mr... Lady Anne Tree, I called last week... You see, I'm terribly eager that he drop by the embroidery workshop, sooner rather than later. The thing is it's going rather... Well yes, I do see he's terrifically busy but unless he actually visits he won't be able to give us a report, and without a report the funding will... We're on a trial, that's the thing. Fine Cell Work. *(controlling frustration)* I have left my number. Several times. A mobile phone?! No! How about I call back this afternoon? Tomorrow? Try writing? Yeeees. I did try that. Still waiting. Although that's not to say I couldn't write again. And to you.

She hangs up, utterly frustrated.

Fuck it!

To calm herself, ANNE *picks up an old diary and flicks through. She reads aloud.*

"We are moored in water lilies and lotus. Kingfishers are everywhere. Some kites and lots of duck and geese. In the evening Sultan gave us a feast. We ate on the floor and our tablecloth was decorated with Welcome Big Ladyship spelt out in flowers. It was extremely uncomfortable, and the food was disgusting – balls of mutton fat impregnated with rosemary. But Michael, luckily, had thought to bring along whisky from the duty free, and so we washed it down." Good idea.

ANNE *pours herself a drink and knocks it back.*

Namaste.

ANNE *then sits at her desk and types, fast, two fingers.*

In Iceland, where I was lucky enough to once go on a birdwatching trip, there were fishermen knitting... I bought jerseys for my daughters, so warm, and a rather fetching hat, and there was no question of minding about the price, the work was beyond beautiful...

On the wall we see the words highlighted. The sound of her typing continues.

Scene Twenty-One

Prison.

Lights up on wing. **BUSBY** *has a broom and is chasing something across the floor.* **LEN** *hovers with a dustpan.* **KEITH** *watches them, nervous, his back to the wall.*

BUSBY Bastard's getting away. Hang on, there's the other one.

LEN I nearly had him, the little swine.

BUSBY Stay there. I'll run them down. Then we can boil them up for soup.

KEITH That's it. It's not in my job remit to work with vermin. No offence, I'm talking about the rats.

LEN Mice. I'm sure of it.

KEITH I've already warned them. I'm not doing it. I'm not paid enough for this.

LEN Hold still. Ahhh, nearly had him then.

Gets down on his hands and knees.

Sometimes if you catch them by the tail. Open a window and sling 'em out.

BUSBY Yeah. That's the thing. Open a window!

KEITH Just get on with it. There must be a bucket somewhere.

LEN A bucket. Are you mad? They'll jump out. Like kangaroos, they are. Get superpowers on the food that we can't stomach.

KEITH Right, that's it.

He blows his whistle.

BUSBY Come on, Gov. Don't go. Any more staff out and we'll be on bang-up for God knows how long.

KEITH *(shouts to someone offstage)* Lock me out will you. I'm coming through.

KEITH *runs the length of the wing and is gone.*

BUSBY Come on, you little beasts. Let's be having you.

LEN Come on, you buggers.

BUSBY Better make the most of this. It'll be the last exercise you'll be having for some time. *(pause)* How's your sponsored run coming?

LEN Not bad. I've run 510 miles.

BUSBY How much you raised now?

LEN Fifty p. *(stops)* Last time it was three weeks before the officers came back. Who cares about a few little mice.

BUSBY Len. You know they're rats. And if no one walks out, nothing gets done. Twenty-three-hour bang-up for us all.

Scene Twenty-Two

Sewing room.

ANNE *sorting out her bag. She holds up* **LUKASZ**'*s finished dog.*

ANNE Beautifully done, and on the back too.

KEITH *puts his head in.*

KEITH Do you mind me asking, was it you used to visit Myra Hindley?

ANNE *(taken aback)* It was.

KEITH Why would you do something like that?

ANNE If you believe in compassion – and her name came up on the rosta – that has to extend to everyone. Now, where are my men? Don't tell me?

KEITH Health and safety.

ANNE *(maddened)* And there was actually a chance of the Governor calling by today!

KEITH If you want a tip-off, you can save yourself the trouble of coming in next week and all.

ANNE I'll be here.

ANNE *lays out coloured thread.* **KEITH** *picks up the dog. Sees label.*

KEITH *(genuinely surprised)* Pietrowski? He made this?

ANNE I was thinking it might be nice to encourage whoever buys it to write to the stitcher – a word of appreciation.

KEITH Yeah? And how many embroidery-loving, criminal sympathising, letter-writing people are out there, do you think?

ANNE Legions!

KEITH Pietrowski. Any idea what he's in for?

ANNE No. And it's none of my business.

KEITH Thirteen years. He didn't steal a loaf of bread.

ANNE I've always believed that everyone deserves a second chance.

KEITH *looks at her.*

Well, almost everyone.

She continues sorting through her bag.

The most haunting thing – she kept pictures of the children in her cell. "To help repent," she said. But it was clear to me, to everyone, they were there as trophies.

To distract herself, **ANNE** *pulls new designs from her bag.*

Once I had my daughters, I couldn't visit any more. She showed no pity, that's the thing. And if you show no pity...

She holds up an image of a turtle drawn onto linen.

KEITH Unusual.

ANNE My husband and I...we used to... We were lucky enough to see some wonderfully out-of-the-way places...

She looks at the image herself.

The Galapagos.

She holds up another. A ship leaning into the wind.

KEITH We had a trip planned. The wife and I, but she's...moved in with her sister. So unless she's back by August I'll be in Cornwall, caravanning on my own.

The light goes off. No one moves to punch it on.

Said she didn't think I'd notice.

ANNE Marriage. It can be most awfully trying.

KEITH I had so much overtime, I *didn't* notice, not for three days.

ANNE Sometimes not noticing can be what saves a marriage.

KEITH Why are you in here? Are you religious?

ANNE It's not terribly popular – this idea of compassion – at least when I was growing up, it was as if the Empire would fall if you showed an ounce of it. Letting the side down, courting disaster. Not religious, no, but I always knew, even as a child, I sided with the underdog.

KEITH I was thinking of writing to one of those agony aunt people, in the paper.

ANNE Best not.

KEITH She thinks I've been in here too long.

ANNE Say nothing. Keep smiling. And remember that you liked each other once, chances are you may like each other again.

ANNE *punches on the light. They smile at each other.*

ANNE *holds up an image of a thistle.*

KEITH Do you ever get them to do their own designs? The inmates?

ANNE It may surprise you to know, it's one thatched cottage after another. It's what dreams are made of.

ANNE *starts to stitch.*

KEITH *(looks at watch)* I'd better get on. There's a new lad on B wing. Suicide watch. And remember, no point coming in next week.

KEITH *exits.*

ANNE *(calls after him)* Fingers crossed that she comes back. Your wife.

She sits sews in a low light through the next scene.

Scene Twenty-Three

Prison. Night.

TOMMY *and* **LUKASZ** *lie in their bunks, listening to the wailing and shouting of a* **MADDENED PRISONER.** *Other* **PRISONERS** *join in. The bars rattle. The doors are kicked.*

LUKASZ *begins to sing, anything to keep himself sane.*

LUKASZ

SŁONECZKO ZASZŁO, CZYLI ZAGASŁO,
I JUZ SIE SCIEMNIA, PRZED WIECZOREM.

Faster and louder.

W ZIELONYM GAJU, PTASZKI SPIEWAJA

(picking up his sewing, examining it) I'm nearly finish of materials and then what I do? What I do then?

TOMMY *(pulls a sheaf of wool from inside his trousers)* What will you give me for this little haul?

LUKASZ *(appalled)* Whole sewing class could be stop because of you.

TOMMY Throw in a bag of bacci and a couple of phonecards and we're talking. I've got forest green. Got to be worth something?

LUKASZ You nasty piece of work. When you come in, you not so bad. But now, you monster.

TOMMY Deal?

LUKASZ *jams his hand down and breaks his needle. Now he is in a real fury.*

LUKASZ Tell me you thieve needle too?

He draws out his knife and presses it against **TOMMY**'s *neck.*

No? You useless?

Turning away he stabs the knife into the mattress, rips photos off the walls. After a moment **TOMMY** *joins him. They tip over the bed, smash up the table, pull the basin away from the wall. They are happy while they destroy everything they can. When it is done they stand amid the wreckage. Even they are stunned.*

Interval

ACT TWO

Scene One

ANNE *sits in a small recording booth. She has head phones on and is doing a radio interview.*

ANNE During the war. I was working, at Eastbourne, in the army canteen and I was struck by it, how the men that had a bit of sewing to do, socks to darn, mending... Well yes – the seed of the idea certainly. It was at Eastbourne that I...formed a friendship you could say, with a cousin of mine, we were terribly young, although...well, he was most awfully keen on me. And then he was killed, died in the sand dunes outside Caan. And when it happened, it was the most extraordinary thing, even before the letter came I saw it in a dream, his smiling face, and he was gone. And then my eldest brother, Billy, shot by a sniper. That's when I started stitching.

Scene Two

Prison cell. It has been put back together.

TOMMY *is drawing on the wall. Another month to add to the ones that are there.* **LUKASZ** *is on his bunk, sewing, the chintz quilt draped over the edge.*

LUKASZ I strongest man in all prison, and now...best quilter! You want I try teach you?

TOMMY I don't fucking need anyone to teach me.

LUKASZ Lady Anne, she say she miss you. She say you reminding her of someone.

TOMMY Some other dickhead loser. How much you getting paid for that?

LUKASZ If I paid one hundred pound and stitch three hundred squares – how much I getting for one square?

TOMMY Leave off. No, hang on.

Does sums on wall.

If it was one hundred squares, that's one pound. Then divided by three...for three hundred. *(gives up)* How many still to go?

LUKASZ I want to make this quilt same size as cell. Eight feet by six.

TOMMY *writes 8x6 on his hand.*

TOMMY You want to rent some out? If you pay me a pound a square.

LUKASZ What happen divide by five?

TOMMY Alright, fifty pence.

LUKAS Ha! Twenty.

TOMMY Forty.

LUKASZ Thirty-five.

TOMMY Bastard.

LUKASZ Deal.

TOMMY *climbs up onto the bed beside* **LUKASZ.**

You remembering what you learn?

LUKASZ *hands him a square, folds back the sleeve of his T-shirt and we see a row of needles. He chooses him one.*

We use running stitch. No knot!

They smile at each other and they sew.

You have news from girlfriend?

TOMMY Shhh. You're distracting me. Have to rethread my bloody needle now.

LUKASZ She still cross?

TOMMY Cross? When I get out... If I get out, she wants a restraining order on me. I'd say she was cross. And you? You never say nothing about your family.

LUKASZ I speak, I cry. I not want to cry.

TOMMY Fair enough.

Pause.

LUKASZ Three girls. One boy. *(blinks)* You see?

TOMMY Why they never visit?

LUKASZ No visit! That my challenge. They asking to come. They say they find a way. Like me. Smuggling out from Poland. But I say no.

TOMMY What you doing here anyway?

LUKASZ Here? Or here? *(pause)* I earning money. More money in one month than I getting in one year. I live in empty house, sleep in...bag on floor. Four men, and me. We send everything for wife. For home. One night I wake, and Igor, he sleep by door, is gone. My bag, my tools, I keep always close, is also gone. I am up. I run through streets. And I see him, Igor, and one friend. "Return to me my belongings..." But they not return, they fight, and I fight too, and I strike. Igor, he is running, and other man, he fall and he crack skull on step. Finish. Not straight away but... Then I am finish too.

TOMMY Why don't they send you back?

LUKASZ Sure. They wishing to deport me. But Poland, they not want me. Soldiers in the street, soldiers in the woods. No work. No food. No nothing. One day we come part of Europe. Then maybe I going home.

TOMMY Clippers please.

LUKASZ You done?

He inspects a square.

No bad. If I know you so fast I would have stuck at 20 pence.

TOMMY Right, which one shall I do next?

Flicks through squares.

Garden Party. Honeysuckle Chintz.

LUKASZ Don't be moron. Is Passionflower. See?

TOMMY I quite fancy Kashmir Leaf.

LUKASZ You want trouble? I make trouble.

TOMMY Alright! Passionflower. I got it.

Lights dim. They remain stitching.

Scene Three

The recorded static of a radio builds as we hear the different politicians talking about the state of prisons.

We hear **ANNE***'s voice from before.*

ANNE And then my eldest brother, Billy, shot by a sniper in Belgium. That's when *I* started stitching...

RADIO VOICE Prison works. It ensures that we are protected from murderers, muggers and rapists – and it makes many who are tempted to commit crime think twice. This may mean that more people will go to prison. We must not flinch from that. We shall no longer judge the success of our system of justice by a fall in our prison population.

RADIO VOICE 2 If you don't want the time, don't do the crime.

RADIO VOICE 3 "I've got my rights," is the verbal equivalent of two fingers to authority. Are we saying that we want the balance of justice tipped in favour of the criminal and the wrongdoer, rather than the victim and the law abider?

RADIO VOICE 1 The unreasonable demands of prisoners have come under increasing criticism... The privileges, the luxury...

RADIO VOICE 2 How come life in prison doesn't mean life? Stop thinking in terms of "punishment" think instead of safeguarding innocent people.

RADIO VOICE 3 It may be true that England and Wales has the highest imprisonment rate in Western Europe, but let us not be ashamed of that.

RADIO VOICE 4 And now the highest suicide rate per capita of prison population.

Scene Four

Lights back up on prison cell. A few weeks later.

TOMMY *and* **LUKASZ** *stand triumphant at either end of the cell and hold the quilt out as wide as they can. An explosion of chintz flowers. It covers the whole floor space. Music fades away.*

TOMMY So when do I get my cash?

LUKASZ That takes time.

TOMMY Everything in this place takes time!

The men start folding the quilt.

LUKASZ But it come. Through system. And then you having funds.

TOMMY Yeah? And how much is our Ladyship getting paid? What kind of salary is she on?

LUKASZ She paid nothing. She come because she...

TOMMY What's her angle then?

LUKSASZ ...I don't know why she come.

TOMMY Everyone got an angle. It's what my dad taught me, when I was eight years old. Can't trust your left hand from your right.

LUKASZ He tell you that before or after he running off.

TOMMY He disappeared. I told you. Through a crack in the ground. They searched for him, the police and all. What you making next? I could give you a hand if you're stuck.

LUKASZ No subletting. You do own project.

TOMMY *(shakes quilt out)* What about we turn this quilt into a floor plan of the cell. We put the bunk along here. The chairs. Table. The bog.

LUKASZ Miss Anne selling to smart people for bed cover. No one wanting to know the size of two men's world.

TOMMY I got a T-shirt. We could cut it into strips, stitch on the outlines. Like a chalk drawing.

LUKASZ Like crime scene.

TOMMY *pulls a T-shirt from a small cupboard and attacks it with his teeth. No luck. He wrenches it but it's hard to break through the seam.*

TOMMY Cheese Baron got hold of a mobile phone last week. Must be possible to get scissors. Although I wouldn't want to be the geezer who smuggled them in.

LUKASZ Give here.

LUKASZ *pulls from the neck and manages to rip the T-shirt. A long strip.*

LUKASZ See, strongest man in prison!

TOMMY *(examines strip)* It'd be nice to have it neat.

LUKASZ You have things for trade?

TOMMY I've got nothing.

LUKASZ *continues ripping up the T-shirt.* **TOMMY** *joins him. They start marking the outlines of the cell.*

We could put the loo roll in. Your slippers.

LUKASZ *(quiet)* Perfection not usually expected...

TOMMY I was thinking...if I could write to Kelly, at a friend's or something. But I've not written a letter, I wouldn't know what to say.

LUKASZ Ask that she send photo.

TOMMY Fuck off.

LUKASZ In Poland, they allow visit, keep men sane, conjugoogal right.

TOMMY Get back there now!

LUKASZ Len. He writing good letter. I write good letter, but your girl, maybe she not read Polish.

TOMMY That'd be pushing it, but she is clever. Done well at school. I stopped going, didn't I...when my Dad...when he...

LUKSAZ Pass cotton. We use overstitch, yes?

They sew.

So what you say, in letter?

TOMMY *(thinks)* Listen, Kel, what I need you to do...pick up the phone, call the solicitor, tell him...

LUKASZ Keep sweet. Slow.

TOMMY I miss you, Kelly.

LUKASZ Is good.

TOMMY I miss you so much.

LUKASZ Is too good.

TOMMY You're not going to believe it. I did a bit of sewing. I made a butterfly, I'll send it to you if... I'm sorry, Kel.

LUKASZ Three cigarette.

TOMMY What's that?

LUKASZ That what he charging. For letter.

TOMMY Len? I thought he was running the length of Britain to cure lung cancer. That's me fucked. I've got nothing.

Scene Five

ANNE *walks across the front of the stage. She is looking for her dog.*

ANNE Biscuits.

She pats her pocket. As she searches, **TOMMY** *and* **LUKASZ** *join the* **OTHER MEN** *in a series of repetitive movements. Lying down. Sitting up. Running on the spot. Press-ups. Pull-ups. Making beds. Flushing toilets. Heads in hands.*

Guuuuzzle. Guzzle! Where have you got to?

A mobile phone rings in her pocket. As she attempts to answer it she switches it off.

Honestly. Damn thing.

It rings again.

Lady Anne Tree. *(furious)* Absolutely not! He said this month... But I was promised...! And it's not just these men that are being repeatedly let down, what about the other sixty-five thousand convicted... Yes, I did read about the government's plans for new, bigger prisons by the year 2000 but I really don't see how this... *(controls herself with difficulty)* You'll write to me, will you? I can't say I shall be holding my breath.

She struggles to switch it off. It beeps and rings. She remembers the dog.

Guzzle! GUZZLE!

Behind her **KEITH** *marches down the corridor.*

KEITH The Chelsea boys *(celtic boys)* we are here, to fuck your women and drink your beer.

Scene Six

Prison. The sewing room.

TOMMY *and* **LUKASZ** *stand on chairs attempting to hang up the quilt which is now an exact replica of their cell. They are watched by* **LEN, BUSBY** *and* **DENISE**.

TOMMY Too high. That's it. Bit more. Bit more.

LUKASZ Cloth heavy. Tape not strong.

TOMMY You should have seen Old Clarkey's face when I asked for tacks and a hammer.

ANNE *enters carrying her trademark bags.* **TOMMY** *and* **LUKASZ** *give up on the tape and hold the quilt up.*

LUKASZ Is our cell. Me and The Kid.

ANNE *comes close and stares at it.*

TOMMY Will you be able to sell it? With the bog an' all?

ANNE *(inspects it closely)* I was reading, just the other day... there's going to be an exhibition. The history of quilts. If I could get a commission for you to stitch a prison quilt.

Stares at quilt again.

It's nice to see they've finally got proper working lavs in this prison. *(back to men)* One of the quilts that is being shown was stitched by convicts in 1840 on their way to Australia. It's being brought back to hang at the V&A.

LUKASZ What is this V and A?

ANNE Do any of you... Have any of you been to the Victoria and Albert Museum?

No one has.

Each man could make a square, about what prison means to you.

BUSBY As long as it's not artichokes.

LEN Boredom, that's the killer.

BUSBY When I was first inside, there was no one to help me with my wheelchair. For six months I didn't leave my cell.

DENISE It's the loneliness that gets me.

TOMMY Once, when I was a kid, I went to the Science Museum with school.

ANNE Just along the road, between Kensington and Knightsbridge.

BUSBY It's about survival, isn't it?

DENISE I sleep with one eye open.

TOMMY So many old people. I wasn't expecting that.

LEN It's the noise that drives me mad.

LUKASZ In prison library there is a book with photos. Clock face of Big Ben, Henry Eight – cellar fill with wine, and here, centre hall with spurs running off. Unseen London.

LEN Unseen. But not by us.

LUKASZ We make quilt, same design.

BUSBY What, so you got the ground floor with the central hall...

Moves across the space in his wheelchair, trailing yarn behind him.

One, two, three...

The other four men mark out the points. **ANNE** *takes the fifth side.* **BUSBY** *drops his shoe on the sixth.*

...four, five, six.

ANNE A hexagon.

BUSBY Five spurs, that's corridors, leading away, each to their own wing... And above – the twos – the second floor, three more spurs with wings.

There is a mesh of coloured wool across the stage.

LEN We could do blanket stitch for bricks.

BUSBY Scroll stitch for wire.

DENISE Satin stitch for walls.

LUKASZ Basket stitch for bars.

TOMMY Chain stitch for...chains?

ANNE *(surveying the chaotic floor plan)* It's going to be a lot of work. Take a lot of time.

LUKASZ We not going nowhere.

Light goes out.

DENISE Seems to be that way.

BUSBY *(swings round and thumps on the light)* We're staying right here, whether you want us to or not!

LEN Will you be part of the quilt, Lady Anne?

ANNE No, Len. But thank you. It'll be all yours.

The lights dim.

Scene Seven

There is the sound of gunshot. Projected we see birds rise into the air. We pick out ANNE*'s face, alarmed.*

ANNE Michael. Oh Lord. Guzzle.

There is the cawing sound of crows.

Scene Eight

Back to the men. As the lights rise we see they are now all embroidering images onto white pieces of cloth, wearing women's glasses. They stitch in unison, leaning a little to the side, making big loops with the thread.

LEN Last night when I put on my new glasses, threaded this needle without going cross-eyed, I had to ask myself, how did she do it? How did you do it, Lady Anne?

ANNE Put the word out at the Women's Institute. Sorry the frames are...

LEN No. How did you get permission for...this?

ANNE There were times when I felt like giving up. Fired off letter after letter, and when no one took a blind bit of notice, in a moment of pure fury, one last letter to the Home Office of such rudeness...

LEN Bet you don't know the meaning of the word.

ANNE It had been a bugger of a week...

ANNE *takes off her jacket and lays it on a chair next to* **TOMMY.**

Another proposal rebuffed...another petition batted into the long grass... another snide remark about my *passion for tatting...*

LUKASZ Tell us how you rude or I let the back of my embroidery go messy!

DENISE Out with it, Lady Anne.

ANNE *(standing)* "No wonder our country is going to the dogs with shits like you in charge."

The all cheer.

I had our driver deliver it by hand – I wasn't having that old chestnut about it being lost in the post! Then – Nothing. Just a note, addressed, not to me, but to my husband.

TOMMY *slips his hand into the pocket of* **ANNE**'*s jacket and slides out the small key.*

That's when I did give up. Several years passed – and I happened to be at a party, where I was introduced to a young man. Anne Tree?! He worked at the Home Office. He told me that when they were bored – he was rather a young man – they sometimes took my letters out and read them. "*...with shits like you...*" That one had been framed and was hanging in the lav! It was a turning point. I'm not saying it was overnight but slowly, slowly, I managed to convince the powers that be it was perfectly natural for men to sew.

DENISE Natural as childbirth.

BUSBY Tinker, *tailor...*

LEN soldier...

DENISE sailor.

LEN Rich man, poor man,

TOMMY Beggar man.

BUSBY *(looks at* **TOMMY***)* Thief.

Fade to black.

Scene Nine

Light picks out one man at a time, as **TOMMY** *moves between them.*

TOMMY *stands before* **LEN**. *He holds out the key.*

TOMMY What's it worth to you?

LEN *(whispering)* My grandkid's getting christened. There's a chance...maybe for an afternoon, they might let me out on home leave.

TOMMY Yeah, but you could...

LEN Fuck off!

LEN *turns his back on him.*

Lights dim, come up on **DENISE**. **DENISE** *takes the key. Dangles it against her ear.*

DENISE Lovely. You got another one?

TOMMY There are six pairs of scissors in that cupboard. What you want to trade?

DENISE I don't do anything without protection.

TOMMY No, that's not...

DENISE Although...if you're desperate...you can suck my cock.

TOMMY *attempts to grabs the key.*

What did you think? That I was going to stage a protest. Force them to close the wing until they sign my form? You confusing me with another Lady. We're not all the same, you know.

Lights dim. Come up on **LUKASZ**.

LUKASZ Sure, I take it.

TOMMY What will I get?

LUKASZ You get what is coming to you.

TOMMY I could try the Barons. Worth a lot, scissors.

LUKASZ You think you smart?

TOMMY Worth even more, a knife.

LUKASZ You fool.

A sharp whistle. The men all freeze, except **BUSBY** *who wheels past* **TOMMY** *and whips the key out of his hand.*

Scene Ten

Lights up on **ANNE** *and* **KEITH** *walking along the corridor.* **KEITH** *locking and unlocking doors. Sound effects of clanging metal.*

KEITH If you feel yourself to be in danger...

ANNE There's never been any trouble...

KEITH Stick your fingers in their eyes.

ANNE ...and I don't recall anything rum going on.

KEITH Or failing that, grab them by the balls, and squeeze.

ANNE I should have checked.

KEITH *stops. Faces her.*

KEITH When it comes down to it, it's either you or them.

ANNE I always keep it here. *(pats pocket)* I just don't see how...

They reach the sewing room.

Scene Eleven

The men look up at them. Silence.

ANNE The room hasn't been cleaned, as usual, so if it's here...

KEITH If it's here!

ANNE *starts searching, looking in corners, under chairs.*

ANNE There's no sign of it.

KEITH We have a problem. A problem of the missing item variety. To be precise, the...haberdashery cupboard key has gone missing.

The men remain silent.

You have three minutes for it to miraculously re-appear or you'll all be going down the block

Silence.

No? Or maybe you'd prefer I lock you in the shower room. Leave you to sort it out amongst yourselves.

Another silence.

Right. You know the drill. Strip, squat, cough.

The men line up, murmuring their protest.

(to **ANNE***)* If you could step outside.

LEN With all due respect, Gov, can I remind you of Article 10 of the International Covenant on Civil and Political Rights, which dictates that in order to preserve dignity prisoners must be allowed to undress one section at a time? First the top half will be exposed...

KEITH Enough of your lip. NOW! *(to* **BUSBY***)* And you.

ANNE *(despairing)* The thing is I really do believe we were finally about to get that wretched report...

KEITH *(glares at her)* Report? There'll be a report all right... chances are this entire wing will have to be locked down.

As **ANNE** *walks towards the door,* **BUSBY** *nudges* **LEN** *and hands him the key.* **LEN** *passes it along to* **LUKASZ** *who passes it to* **DENISE** *who passes it to* **TOMMY. TOMMY** *pulls off his shirt fast, and flings the shirt towards* **ANNE.** *The key appears at her feet. She stoops to pick it up – with difficulty – then turns on* **TOMMY,** *who she is about to berate, but she is struck by the dark red-cuts on both his arms. Instead she clasps her hand to her pocket.*

ANNE I've found it!

Everyone stops.

Sorry gentlemen. My mistake. How idiotic. Do forgive me. It must have slipped into the lining.

KEITH *takes the key, suspiciously, carefully, where has it really been? He unlocks the cupboard. Everything is in place.*

KEITH If anything like this happens again, this particular activity will be closed down with immediate effect.

The men begin dressing.

ANNE *(tight-lipped)* We'd better get on.

KEITH You've been warned, you hear me?

He looks at **ANNE.**

Remember what I said.

He mimes grabbing their balls.

You or them!

KEITH *leaves the room.* **ANNE** *opens her bag and starts taking out thread and material. The men take their seats, sewing in unison. All in a row, to one side, big loops.* **LUKASZ** *starts to hum.*

LEN Shut it, Poland. You're putting me off.

There is silence. Then **LUKASZ** *starts again.*

LUKASZ

SLONECZKO ZASZLO, CZYLI ZAGASLO
I JUZ SIE SCIEMNIA, PRZED WIECZOREM.

ANNE *takes two white hexagons and presses the sides together, talking loudly over the song.*

ANNE The stitches need to be invisible, as tiny as you can make them, neat as a pin. Back stitch is ideal, as close to the edge as you can get without a risk of fraying, so that then, when you turn the cloth over... *(She does this.)* the material can be pressed and will... *(Her voice falters.)* lie nice and flat.

She takes a square of chintz and dabs at her eyes.

LUKASZ Sorry we making you sad.

ANNE Not at all. Nothing to do with... It's been a bloody awful week, that's all...

ANNE *blows her nose on a square of chintz.*

LEN If anyone's upset you, on the out...

BUSBY Just say the word. Right boys?

LEN You don't spend twenty-one years as a guest of Her Majesty without making a few contacts.

ANNE Thank you, but that won't be necessary. Only myself to blame. The sheep in lamb.

LEN You what?

ANNE I had been warned. More than once. *(She barely controls her grief.)* Ridiculous. He was my husband's dog, you see. Devoted. I do apologise. *(blows her nose)* They were within their rights to shoot.

The men all hang their heads. **LUKASZ** *starts to sing his Polish song as the men continue to sew.* **ANNE** *rummages in her bag. Draws out a letter.*

(to **BUSBY***)* This came for you. It's from someone who bought your double artichoke cushion.

She hands him the letter. He turns away to read it. **ANNE** *attends to some paperwork at the small table.*

TOMMY *(nervously trying to change the subject)* I hear Speedy's off to the Enhanced wing tomorrow.

LUKASZ What I hear, they all grasses on that wing.

LEN I've lost track of the amount of times I've applied for Enhanced, but as long as I'm "In Denial," they turn me down.

LUKASZ I hear they is changing that rule.

LEN If it takes as long as it does to change any other rule, I hope I'm out by then. I've done Anger Management, Victim Bloody Empathy, and they're still attempting to enhance my Thinking Skills.

DENISE You been off on a desert island yet?

LEN Been there. Done that. I voted we eat fattest con first.

LUKASZ They want eat me, but I all muscle.

TOMMY Count yourself lucky you get to go to a desert island. If Lady Anne hadn't fought for me, I'd still be on bang-up, going mental in my cell.

He looks anxiously over at **ANNE***. She returns his look and they hold it for a moment until she notices* **BUSBY** *still facing the wall.*

ANNE Are you alright, Mr Busby?

BUSBY *half turns towards her. He holds out the letter. She takes it and reads.*

"I have been told your name but I do not know who or where you are. What I do know is that you have made something of great beauty and value and I wanted to thank you."

BUSBY *(visibly choked up)* First time I've had a letter. Not since I lost my mam.

ANNE *gently hands the letter back.*

LUKASZ *(to* **TOMMY***)* You in shit!

TOMMY She's got the key back now, hasn't she?

LUKASZ The Barons. They lean on you. You wait.

TOMMY I kept it quiet.

LUKASZ There is no quiet. In here?

TOMMY *puts head in hands.*

They coming for you. Now they know you thief.

ANNE It's clear there is a spot of bother. Are you going to let me in on it?

TOMMY It's nothing, Miss.

ANNE *(angry)* It's not nothing to me, Tommy. To me it's thirty years of being branded a "tiresome woman". Of sticking my nose in where it wasn't wanted. Of waiting for the bloody post. "Surely there's a luncheon you'd rather go to? Wouldn't you be better off fundraising for the village fete?" Thirty years hard labour. And to see it evaporate through one stupid, selfish act...

TOMMY *(standing)* So why didn't you grass me up then?

ANNE That's a good question. And I'm asking it of myself now. Why? Because I've always believed everyone, almost everyone, deserves a second chance.

TOMMY *(taking this in)* Almost everyone. I believe that too.

BUSBY *(still looking at his letter)* This might sound strange, Miss, but I've had some of my best times in prison.

ANNE It might sound strange to you too Busby, but so have I. *(to* **TOMMY***)* So Tommy, let's be clear.

Hands him another square.

Press the two sides together, back stitch, nice and straight. Close to the line, and keep going.

Lights dim.

Scene Twelve

Prison cell.

TOMMY *is searching the cell. He looks under* **LUKASZ**'*s pillow, out of the window, pulls in the string. Nothing. He looks inside several cereal packets. Then he lifts the corner of the bunk bed. Out of the hollow leg slides* **LUKASZ**'*s knife. Just as he is picking it up, the door opens and* **LUKASZ** *enters.*

TOMMY Cheese Baron only wants it for an hour.

LUKASZ You believing that? You believing anything.

LUKASZ *lunges for it. They fight, and he gets it. He runs with it to the window.* **TOMMY** *pulls him back. The knife flies from his hands. They both scrabble for it.* **TOMMY** *seizes it,* **LUKASZ** *grabs him, he turns and the knife stabs* **LUKASZ** *in the chest. They freeze in an embrace.*

TOMMY Poland? Mate.

An alarm thrums in the distance.

Slowly **LUKASZ** *slips down to the floor.*

Scene Thirteen

Prison. Sewing room.

BUSBY *and* **DENISE** *sit alone. After a few minutes* **BUSBY** *wheels himself over and punches on the light.* **LEN** *puts his head round the door.*

LEN Still no news?

DENISE What a fucking tragedy.

BUSBY And they're not letting her send anything in.

BUSBY *scratches his hands.*

LEN I've got something to show her, that's the thing. *(shy)* I've done my own design.

He displays a picture of a thatched cottage, with a path and flowers in the front garden. It fills the room. The men gaze at it. Bask in it.

BUSBY Lady Anne would be very proud.

LEN How are we going to finish the quilt now? Poland was the one knew what he was doing.

BUSBY *(shaking his head)* Not any more.

DENISE Didn't it have to be in by the end of this month?

LEN It's got to be passed. They don't just take any old thing. It may not be up to standard. It's like an exam.

BUSBY *(quoting* **ANNE***)* Perfection is not usually expected of prisoners.

DENISE Where is it anyway?

BUSBY You think the screws got hold of it?

LEN Chances are.

The men sit in dejected silence.

BUSBY How's the running going?

LEN She's in hospital again. Trisha. Whether I keep running or stand still, she's not getting out.

DENISE I'm sorry to hear that.

LEN Seen anything of The Kid?

DENISE No.

BUSBY There's no way up to the twos. Not for me. And I don't go into the yard.

LEN You don't... What never?

BUSBY. I tried it once. Sun on my face. Bit of breeze. Nearly killed me. Easier to stay inside.

What'll he get?

LEN World cups. Don't ask me how many.

DENISE They had to hose the cell down. That much blood.

BUSBY *(scratching hands frantically)* If she doesn't come back...

They sit in silence. Eventually the light goes out.

Scene Fourteen

Prison cell.

TOMMY *stands alone in his cell. It has been stripped of* **LUKASZ***'s things. He drops to the ground and starts doing press-ups.*

TOMMY One for sister, up, one for mother *(unsure)* up, none for father...down, down. One for barsht, one for vodka. One for pickles. Red pepper... Plum...

The shouting starts. Screams from the segregation block. Desperate. Bleak. **TOMMY** *jumps up and attacks the imaginary punch bag.*

One for bit of fucking quiet.

He climbs up on his chair.

Wanker. Fucking shitface. Go on then. Go on. You want to top yourself, why don't you?

PRISONER 1 Shut up you, fraggle.

PRISONER 2 Quiet you, nutter.

PRISONER 1 Useless bastard. Shut the fuck up.

PRISONERS Shut up, shut up, shut up!

*The same voice as before starts singing "****JOLENE****".* **TOMMY** *lifts his shirt and takes out a threaded needle. He lifts it to his mouth and pulls it through his lip, and again so that soon he has three black stitches across his mouth. He stares out, still standing on his chair.*

Scene Fifteen

Prison entrance.

ANNE *has her two big laundry-style bags of wool and kits. She is standing at the security window.* **KEITH** *is behind it.*

ANNE Don't be ridiculous. Here's my pass. I've even got a letter somewhere. Damn, where is it?

KEITH If your name's not on the list.

ANNE It's me. Lady Anne. It must be there.

KEITH If you don't mind I'd ask you to move out of the way.

ANNE *(furious)* But I do mind. There are men inside who rely on seeing me.

KEITH If you don't stand out of the way you'll have to be forcibly removed.

He blows a whistle.

ANNE At least I can leave some materials for the quilt. They'll need more thread, the maroon particularly is very low.

KEITH If you're not on the list, there's nothing we can do.

ANNE Can I not leave some cotton at least...a reel of white. Now, stop all this nonsense, you know perfectly well who I am.

KEITH *looks round, then slides open the window. She passes through cotton and some skeins of coloured thread.*

Am I to assume she's still not back?

KEITH There's going to be a cooling down period, do you hear me? Orders from the top. I'll have to ask you to step away.

KEITH *shuts the window.* **ANNE** *retreats a little, then thinking better of it, sits on her bag. She takes out her floral diary. As she reads we see* **TOMMY** *in his cell, still* *standing on his chair staring into space, his mouth stitched together.*

ANNE "Out at sea, schools of golden rays, scudding through the water with their dark fins showing, three different kinds of shark, pelicans galore, and the most beautiful bird, the common egret, making a swan look like a goose. Never again do I want to see a fish or a turtle in an aquarium. Or anything caged in for that matter. A lovely swim off the boat and a humiliating haul in, with me in my bathing sarong – for the fuller figure – unravelling around me. Thank the Lord I'd kept my underwear on!"

Along the corridor comes **KEITH**, *leading a man with a bedroll under his arm.*

"There were marine iguanas, and red-footed boobies, and then...a party of Germans turned up in a sailing boat. We assumed they were there for the wildlife but they started pointing. 'Typical English.' They were terribly excited, must have thought we were some kind of diminishing species."

She closes the diary.

Is that right, darling, is that what we were?

KEITH *stops outside* **TOMMY**'*s cell, unlocks it and pushes the door open.*

KEITH In you go, son, don't be shy.

The man stands still, staring at **TOMMY**.

Fucking hell.

The **NEW PRISONER** *turns around and bolts, running as fast as he can along the corridor. Whistles blow and bars rattle as he is caught, his hands cuffed behind his back.*

KEITH *enters cell and gently unpicks the stitches in* **TOMMY**'*s mouth.*

What have you done to yourself? I shouldn't be telling you this but there's news in – the extra charges against you

– they've been dropped. I'll get something for... (*He points to his own mouth.*)

KEITH *exits.*

TOMMY *is still holding his mouth, when* **LEN** *comes in carrying* **BUSBY** *on his back.* **BUSBY** *is carrying the nearly finished quilt with* **DENISE** *behind, holding it up like a train.*

LEN We've only got an hour.

He puts **BUSBY** *on a chair.*

We'd better get started. Bloody hell!

They all stare at **TOMMY**.

LEN *shakes out the quilt. Hands them each a corner.*

If we stitch like this every day for one hour. No shower. No phone calls. No exercise. We should have it done by the end of the month.

BUSBY Is this what they call a sewing bee?

DENISE A stitch bitch, I think you'll find.

TOMMY Yeah. And then what? We give it to the screws to brighten up their office?

LEN I've done a deal. *(lowering his voice)* Clarkey, he promised to pass it over. Lady Anne, word is, every Tuesday she waits outside the gate.

KEITH *puts his head round the door. He sees* **LEN** *and there's a look between them. It's clear* **TOMMY** *doesn't need him.*

KEITH Right.

Hands over a letter to **TOMMY** *instead.*

Held up at the censor, but it's been checked and cleared. Eventful day today.

He casts a look at the quilt, then back at **LEN**, *smiles, exits.*

TOMMY *opens his letter.*

TOMMY *(reading, haltingly)* “Is very bad in here.”

Scene Sixteen

Light on **LUKASZ** *in his new cell.*

LUKASZ I not strongest man in this prison. But the time it will pass, whichever way we counting it. My wife, my boy, they not wanting me home. In Poland, I lucky, never getting caught, but in UK my rage is bigger than my brain. Give me back my tools – and the man, he set down my bag. He moving it towards me. But is too late. I want to hurt him. If I don't hurt him I hurting myself. Here, far from country, far from pig father, here is best I stay.

Back to: Scene Fifteen.

Prison cell.

LEN Where'd they send him?

DENISE High security. Isle of Wight.

Out of the envelope **TOMMY** *pulls a quilt piece. He holds it up. It's the image of two hands, clasped in friendship.*

TOMMY Last word from Lukasz. I'll stitch it in myself.

They sew.

What did you have to do to fix this, Len?

DENISE Darling. Don't ask.

LEN Wrote a letter to Mrs Clarke, that's all. Make it saucy, he said. Must have done the trick. Got a smile on his face today.

DENISE And he's working in the kitchen with me. Aren't you, love?

LEN She persuaded me. Better than sitting in my cell if there's no more stitching to be done. And no more running.

TOMMY You given up?

LEN Wednesday. Thought they might let me out for the funeral, but no.

There is a shocked silence. **DENISE** *puts a hand on his shoulder.* **LEN** *doesn't shake it off.*

BUSBY If there's no more stitching...

He begins to scratch his hands.

DENISE Just for the moment.

BUSBY You say that...

TOMMY Yeah...

LEN Do you know Lady Anne? Have you met her?

He stands.

"No wonder our country is going to the dogs..." She'll be back.

Scene Seventeen

V&A.

Lights up on the quilt at the V&A. It is hanging on the wall, a projected impression. **TOMMY** *is in his own clothes. He is carrying a disposable camera, looking at the exhibits, singing* ***"YOUR SONG"*** *by Elton John, quietly to himself. He walks forward and stares up at it.*

ANNE *enters.*

ANNE Tommy, is that you? How wonderful, you're out.

TOMMY GH6732, Miss.

ANNE *(puts out her hand)* It's terrific to see you.

TOMMY I was hoping I'd have a chance to say...if there's ever anything I can do...to...

ANNE Oh but there is. I see you have a camera, and I did so want to take photos. Could you do that for me? And I'll take them into the men.

TOMMY I don't mind what goes in, as long as it's not me.

TOMMY *walks to the centre of the stage. As he does, the back wall lights up section by section, and each square is clearly visible, freedom, dreams, time being counted off, flowers, tattoos, nightmares.*

Our men step forward one by one.

BUSBY Three thousand stitches on an artichoke. Eight hundred on a stalk.

LEN Back stitch. Cross stitch. Chain stitch. Running stitch.

LUKASZ All these years I thinking about my crimes. But with threads in needle, I think of other things.

LEN You can forget you're in a tiny cell with another man. In your head, he's not there.

DENISE Open chain, broad chain, zigzag chain, twisted chain.

BUSBY Two hundred stitches on a snowflake, seven hundred on a star.

LEN When I'm sewing my mind does what I want it to do.

LUKASZ Brain free.

DENISE Emerald, cinnamon, forest green.

LEN Maroon. Burnt umber. Aquamarine.

LUKASZ I not strongest man in this prison.

DENISE. There are forty thousand stitches in an average cushion.

LEN I sent my girls something at Christmas. First time in twenty years.

LUKASZ No stitching here.

The projection disappears.

KEITH *(stepping forward)* Alright everybody. Lock up. NOW!

Everyone except **TOMMY** *and* **ANNE** *scatter.*

TOMMY *(holding out the camera)* I'll trade you for some orange wool, Lady Anne.

ANNE *reaches out and takes his hand.*

ANNE Deal.

End

As the actors come forward to take their bow, words appear on the back wall:

Today there are eighty-five thousand people locked up in our gaols, with waiting lists for every Fine Cell Work group in England and Wales.

Lightning Source UK Ltd.
Milton Keynes UK
UKHW02f1634250518
323231UK00007B/95/P

9 780573 115561